932-
e edge

WITHDRAWN
UNIVERSITY LIBRARY
THE UNIVERSITY OF TEXAS RIO GRANDE VALLEY

LIBRARY
THE UNIVERSITY OF TEXAS
AT BROWNSVILLE
Brownsville, Tx 78520-4991

FROM THE CENTER
TO THE EDGE

FROM THE CENTER TO THE EDGE

The Politics and Policies of the Clinton Presidency

WILLIAM C. BERMAN

ROWMAN & LITTLEFIELD PUBLISHERS, INC.
Lanham • Boulder • New York • Oxford

LIBRARY
THE UNIVERSITY OF TEXAS
AT BROWNSVILLE
Brownsville, Tx 78520-4991

ROWMAN & LITTLEFIELD PUBLISHERS, INC.

Published in the United States of America
by Rowman & Littlefield Publishers, Inc.
4720 Boston Way, Lanham, Maryland 20706
www.rowmanlittlefield.com

12 Hid's Copse Road
Cumnor Hill, Oxford OX2 9JJ, England

Copyright © 2001 by Rowman & Littlefield Publishers, Inc.

All rights reserved. No part of this publication may be reproduced, stored in a
retrieval system, or transmitted in any form or by any means, electronic, mechanical,
photocopying, recording, or otherwise, without the prior permission of the publisher.

British Library Cataloguing in Publication Information Available

Library of Congress Cataloging-in-Publication Data

Berman, William C., 1932–
    From the center to the edge : the politics and policies of the Clinton presidency /
William C. Berman.
        p. cm.
    Includes bibliographical references and index.
    ISBN 0-8476-9614-6 (alk. paper) -- ISBN 0-8476-9615-4 (pbk. : alk. paper)
    1. United States--Politics and government--1993-2001. 2. Clinton, Bill, 1946- 3.
Political culture--United States--20th century. 4. United States--Foreign relations--1993-
5. United States--Economic policy--1993- I. Title.

E885 .B467 2001
979.929'092--dc21

                                                    2001019406

Printed in the United States of America

♾™ The paper used in this publication meets the minimum requirements of American National
Standard for Information Sciences—Permanence of Paper for Printed Library Materials,
ANSI/NISO Z39.48-1992.

Contents

Acknowledgments

Steve Wrinn, executive editor for history and political theory at Rowman & Littlefield, was a constant source of encouragement and good advice while I prepared this manuscript for publication. Lynn Gemmell and Mary Carpenter of Rowman & Littlefield also provided valuable assistance. Historians Robert Cuff and Jacob Vander Meulen provided a searching read and did much to improve the manuscript's flow and organization. Leo Ribuffo, a reader for Rowman & Littlefield, was helpful and encouraging. Professor Stanley Kutler gave informed answers to my questions whenever I sought him out on a particular matter bearing on this project. I alone am responsible for what appears in this book.

My wife, Deborah, was—as always—supportive and sustaining throughout the writing process. As so often in the past, our family cats, Samantha and Mingus, were on the scene to help with the composition.

This work is dedicated to Berneice K. Smith—the first lady of Berea, Ohio—and to Benjamin and Joshua, my grandsons, for whom a bright future beckons.

"Our burden is to give the people a new choice, rooted in old values, a new choice that is simple, that offers opportunity, demands responsibility, gives citizens more say, provides them responsive government—all because we recognize that we are a community, we are all in this together, and we are going up or down together."

Bill Clinton—May 1991

"The era of big government is over."

January 1996

"I did not have sexual relations with that woman, Miss Lewinsky."

January 1998

"There's a lot to be said for showing up every day and trying to push the rock up the hill. . . . If you are willing to win in inches as well as feet, a phenomenal amount of positive things can happen."

Summer 2000

Introduction

When Bill Clinton was sworn in as president on January 20, 1993, Democrats everywhere sighed with relief. Based on his 1992 campaign, Clinton appeared to have a positive and well-thought-out agenda for coping with the myriad social and economic problems that had festered during the Reagan–Bush era. Now, perhaps, he would lay the groundwork for the reestablishment of Democratic hegemony in national politics, which had been lost since Richard Nixon's election in 1968.

As a result of the social, racial, and cultural strife of the 1960s, which later dovetailed with the deeply rooted economic malaise of the Carter years (1977–81), the coalition constituted by Franklin D. Roosevelt had been ripped apart, thereby preparing the way for the Reagan–Bush era in American politics. Throughout the 1980s, Democrats, in their quest of the presidency, lacked both the political means and the agenda to overcome Ronald Reagan's brand of charismatic conservatism. The question thus arose: How could Democrats shape a new and more appealing message in an attempt to revive the party's presidential prospects? Bill Clinton, politically skilled and ideologically ambidextrous, appeared to have the answer. He was the chief messenger of a newly fashioned Democratic alternative to the older and now seemingly discredited liberalism of Lyndon Johnson's Great Society.

After taking power on behalf of an agenda for "change," Clinton soon encountered serious political difficulties, which eventually brought about a congressional Republican resurgence. Nevertheless,

1

while protecting government from "extremist" attacks, he managed to salvage his political career, withstanding even impeachment during his turbulent second term. And thanks to a booming economy and a budget surplus, he was able to push an activist agenda to the fore in a way that eventually created the context for the general election in 2000.

Here, then, is a story, full of ironic twists and turns, of a president whose mixed record of accomplishment and failure illuminates the point that the historical process is never static and that it unfolds in ways that are often unanticipated. In this particular case, the narrative focuses on the possibilities for progress as well as the constraints, personal and institutional, that defined the limits of the achievable in a political era still dominated by Reagan's mistrust of government. Whether Clinton tried to exercise leadership to shift the balance in a different direction and failed to accomplish very much because of the larger political obstacles he faced, or whether he was only too willing to play the cards he was dealt out of a sense of hard political practicality are matters that will be raised in the pages that follow.

This survey, then, explores the politics and public policies of the Clinton administration, analyzing the origins, evolution, and transformation of its program for change as well as the reasons for its various successes and failures in a conservative era. Although the chief focus will be on domestic matters, such as welfare reform, deficit reduction, and the impeachment process, key foreign policy issues, including American relations with Russia and China, along with the conflict in Bosnia and Kosovo, will be discussed in chronological context.

Today, many historians, immersed in the field of social history and cultural studies, consider the study of political history and public policy too old-fashioned or traditional in approach and content to have much merit as a vehicle for advancing our understanding of the past. But political history does matter, especially when it deals with the presidency, the source of major power and influence in the American political system. That office, after all, gives the chief executive, in his capacity as commander in chief, the power to influence the lives and fortunes of millions of people. Moreover, his authority is such that he bears a significant responsibility, along with the Congress, for the workings and functioning of the American economy both at home and internationally.

While I seek to familiarize readers with many of the salient issues, policies, and problems of the Clinton administration, my hope is that they will also use this survey as a springboard for a deeper examination of national politics and public policy at the end of the twentieth century. For that purpose, I have appended a short bibliographical essay outlining the current literature from which this synthetic narrative emerged.

Chapter One

From Little Rock to Washington

William Jefferson Clinton's climb to the presidency was remarkable, given his early background and personal history. Born in Hope, Arkansas, on August 19, 1946, Clinton had a painful childhood: he never knew his father, who died in an auto accident before he was born, and he saw his stepfather abuse his mother. Yet he managed to overcome such obstacles in high school, where he was a good student with an easy and friendly disposition. And while still in high school, he shook hands with President John F. Kennedy, his idol, during a student gathering at the White House. Later, Clinton made his way to Georgetown University, where he was active in campus politics.

Having won a Rhodes scholarship, Clinton went to Oxford University, where he made important and useful contacts with other American Rhodes scholars, such as Robert Reich and Strobe Talbott, who one day would assist him in achieving his goal of becoming president of the United States. In England, Clinton also took part in public protests against the Vietnam War. Very worrisome to him was the fact that his draft board in Arkansas had called him for induction in July 1969. So he arranged a deal with the Reserve Officer's Training Corps (ROTC) at the University of Arkansas, which gave him a deferment from the draft and allowed him to return to England to pursue another year of studies at Oxford. Years later, the issue of his draft deferment (or evasion) surfaced to embarrass him. A letter that he wrote in December 1969 to the commanding officer of that ROTC unit at the University of Arkansas Law School became public during the early weeks of the 1992 presidential campaign. It revealed that despite his earlier stated intention to enroll as a student at the University of Arkansas Law School and to serve in its ROTC unit after completing his work at Oxford, he no longer had any intention of doing either. Having learned that he had received a sufficiently high number in the new draft lottery system to avoid the likelihood of induction, Clinton felt no necessity to keep that earlier commitment, which is why he wrote the letter.

Upon his return from England, Clinton enrolled in Yale Law School, where he met his future wife, fellow law student Hillary Rodham. Following his graduation, Clinton returned to Arkansas to pursue a career in politics. Extremely ambitious, smart, and resourceful, he was a skillful and hardworking campaigner. In his first race for public office, he nearly defeated a longtime Republican congressman in the 1974 midterm election by running a populist-sounding campaign. After making important contacts and networking with key individuals and interest groups in his home state, he was elected attorney general in 1976, and then governor in 1978. Although Clinton lost his bid for reelection in 1980, he won again in 1982 and in three successive races for governor before moving on to Washington in early 1993.

As several of his biographers have noted, Clinton's years as governor revealed political and operational traits that would later carry over to his presidency. For example, when Clinton was elected governor for the first time in 1978, he campaigned as a moderate progressive, seeking modest changes in the tax structure, among other items on his agenda. But Clinton lost his bid for reelection in 1980, ostensibly because he had pushed through the legislature a slight increase in taxes on motor vehicles, in a state where government was viewed with distrust and deep suspicion. After apologizing repeatedly to the voters for that tax hike, he won reelection in 1982 and vowed never again to stray too far from the conservative mainstream in Arkansas, where both political and economic power was highly concentrated in a largely one-party state.

At the same time, he made alliances with powerful business interests throughout Arkansas, including Tyson Foods and the Stephens investment house, whose financial resources he would tap for his future political campaigns, locally and nationally.

Although Clinton willingly accommodated key interest groups from the corporate and business sector located in Little Rock and elsewhere in the state, he also received strong support from black voters, who were among the state's poorest residents. Their loyalty to him was not surprising. From his days as a high school student, Clinton had established a close emotional bond with black Americans. As a young man, he attended black church services and knew the words and music of many African American spirituals. That relationship was unique for a white politician in Arkansas where segregation had been a way of life for many decades.

Reelected governor in 1982, Clinton embraced a carefully contrived centrist agenda, thereby avoiding issues or positions that might remind voters of his seemingly more progressive stance of 1978–80. And while he protected and enhanced his connections with the business and banking community, his policies often angered the membership of the small Arkansas-based AFL-CIO and activists in the minuscule environmental movement. At the same time, Clinton was often indecisive in office, constantly temporizing on legislative matters, while making promises and commitments that he could not keep or had no intention of keeping. Such behavior created suspicions among fellow politicians and informed reporters that he was neither fully trustworthy nor very reliable.

Hillary Rodham Clinton was more direct in her dealings with people. Playing a key role as an adviser and political strategist, she was a formidable presence and was taken seriously by friends and foes alike. Raised in an upper middle-class Republican household just outside of Chicago, she later graduated from Wellesley College and then Yale Law School, where she met her future husband. Marrying him in October 1975, she fully supported her husband's political career. Together, they became partners in power; each was tied to the other as they pursued their respective goals of political, economic, and personal advancement, aided always by strategically placed friends in the business community. In actual practice, their partnership was a joint division of labor: Bill worked on the public side of things, and Hillary immersed herself in private legal matters and details as a partner at the prestigious Rose Law Firm in Little Rock while keeping tabs on their real estate investment in the Whitewater estates and representing the interests of Madison Guaranty Savings and Loan of Little Rock.

Meanwhile, developments occurring on the national political stage were shaping Bill Clinton's future career. Most important was the overwhelming reelection of Ronald Reagan in 1984, a result that spooked many moderate Democrats, including Georgia Senator Sam Nunn and Tennessee Senator Al Gore. They believed that unless the party changed its message and course, it was doomed to experience more defeats in future presidential elections. Wanting to shift ideological gears and to change the party's identity, they saw the need to challenge the power of the so-called special interest groups in the party, such as organized labor and the cultural left, for whom Jesse Jackson was a major spokesman. Thus, their program included welfare reform, a tougher stance on crime, and a smaller governmental bureaucracy. Such an agenda, they believed, might give the Democratic Party an opportunity to outflank the Republicans on social issues, including crime and welfare, as well as to refute the Republican charge that Democrats were only "tax and spend" liberals.

The Democratic Leadership Council (DLC), founded in 1985 with the help of corporate funding, was the vehicle centrist Democrats used in an attempt to woo back white voters alienated by the cultural liberalism and big government ethos of the national Democratic Party. Those voters had deserted the national Democratic Party in droves during recent presidential elections because they viewed it as being too friendly to blacks and too soft on defense and national security matters. (Earlier, George Wallace, the longtime governor of Alabama, had exploited their frustrations and rage when he ran for president in 1968 and 1972. His campaigns, along with those of Richard Nixon, provided disgruntled Democrats with a way out of the Democratic Party, which quickly worked to the advantage of the GOP.)

As one of the DLC founders, Bill Clinton shared the centrist approach to politics and policy that the DLC embodied, and he would later use the organization as a springboard to launch his bid for the presidency. But his first priority was to retain a viable political base in Arkansas. He was reelected governor in 1982, 1984, and 1986 with the help of consultant Dick Morris, who fashioned for him a permanent campaign strategy for winning those elections, and who later would play such an important role in his presidency. Morris emphasized the need for constant voter polling in order to shape and manipulate policy debates, and he recommended the use of paid media advertising to overcome objections to any of Clinton's policies emanating from the Arkansas press. Also, Morris advised Clinton to couch his idealistic appeals to the voters in such a way that they appeared to support moderate policies and vice versa. In that vein, Clinton addressed the woeful state of public education in his home state and scored a key legislative success by obtaining increased public spending at the expense of forcing teacher groups to undergo competency tests.

At the same time, Clinton's attention was drawn to larger national affairs. Bored with small-scale issues in his home state, and eager to find a way out of Little Rock into the vastly bigger and more exciting world of Washington politics, he often spoke at various forums and meetings, including the National Governors Association, on a variety of public policy issues, such as job creation, welfare, and education reform. There and elsewhere, Clinton impressed important national reporters with his command of the material and eloquent rhetorical style.

As the 1988 election approached, Clinton thought about running for the presidency, especially after former Colorado Senator Gary Hart—the Democratic front-runner—had withdrawn from the race for the party's nomination as a result of a news story highlighting his extramarital affair. But since rumors abounded that Clinton himself was a compulsive philanderer, he was fearful of repeating Hart's fate; so he decided at the last moment not to seek the nomination, using the pretext that he did not wish to subject his wife and young daughter to the hazards of a national political campaign.

Several nationally known Democrats sought the party's nomination in 1988, including Governor Michael Dukakis of Massachusetts, Senator Al Gore of Tennessee, Congressman Richard Gephardt of Missouri, and Jesse Jackson, spokesman for the Rainbow Coalition. After scoring decisive victories in most of the key primaries around the country, Dukakis wrapped up the nomination and headed for Atlanta, the site of the party's convention. There, Clinton placed Dukakis's name in nomination, but his lengthy and tedious speech caused delegates to call for the use of "the hook" in order to end their misery and boredom.

Clinton's speech was the least of Dukakis's problems. Put simply, Dukakis lacked a serious programmatic alternative to the conservative agenda of Ronald Reagan and George Bush during a period of sustained economic growth and the apparent ending of the Cold War. In addition, he was a weak campaigner vulnerable to a devastating Republican assault on sensitive cultural matters such as capital punishment and protection of the flag. And finally, he was handicapped by Jesse Jackson's refusal to move offstage once the campaign began in earnest, a refusal that further alienated Reagan Democrats who hated both Jackson and his agenda.

Bill Clinton was quick to learn from Dukakis's experience. In the event he sought and won the Democratic presidential nomination in 1992, he was determined not to let George Bush and the GOP do to him what they did to Dukakis. After winning reelection as governor of Arkansas in 1990 for the last time, Clinton was now ready to move into the national political arena, having established himself as something of a national figure. In 1986 he was elected president of the National Governors Association; in 1990 he assumed the chair of the DLC, moving him a further step up the ladder into the national arena. And in that capacity, he addressed major national issues from the perspective of a New Democrat who sought to promote a shift in party policy on welfare and the role of government. For Clinton the name of the game was to use government to connect personal responsibility with individual opportunity in order to promote the common good. And like his fellow associates in the DLC, he favored a tougher stance on crime, a middle-class tax cut, welfare reform, and policies to spur economic growth. While presenting his views in a major policy address to the DLC in Cleveland in the spring of 1991, Clinton gave such a polished and powerful speech that it buried memories of his poor performance in Atlanta.

On October 31, 1991, Clinton announced in Little Rock that he was a candidate for the Democratic nomination. Running as a Washington outsider, he remarked that "People out here don't care about the idle rhetoric of 'left' and 'right' and 'liberal' and 'conservative' and all the other words that have made our politics a substitute for action." Along with effective rhetoric, Clinton had adequate funding and a solid organization to help him. And, most important, he also had good luck and timing on his side.

Ironically, George Bush's sweeping and popular victory in the Gulf War contributed greatly to Clinton's future prospects. After Bush's well-organized coalition had driven Saddam Hussein out of Kuwait, he stood at an unprecedented 90 percent in the polls in the winter of 1991, thus appearing unbeatable in his bid for reelection. For this reason, several potentially competitive candidates for the Democratic nomination, such as House Majority Leader Richard Gephardt and Senator Al Gore, decided not to enter the race, thereby opening the door for Clinton to make his mark against lesser rivals and contenders in the party. In addition, the economy, still in a recession, would become the hot-button issue in 1992.

The economy, after all, was a card Democrats had played well for years. Coming out of the 1930s and World War II, they largely benefited from memories of the Depression, allowing them to keep intact a New Deal coalition that had dominated national politics since Franklin Roosevelt's days. But as a result of the Vietnam War and internal party strife arising from the cultural wars and racial conflict of the 1960s and 1970s, that coalition eventually fell apart. Yet the Republicans were unable to capitalize fully on that development until the combination of high inflation and high unemployment converged during the Jimmy Carter years to discredit the widely held belief that the Democrats were better managers of the economy than the GOP. Thus, Ronald Reagan's success in 1980 was built largely on Carter's failure to overcome the blight of stagflation as well as his inability to obtain the release of the fifty-three American hostages held in Teheran.

The Reagan years had consolidated the Republican grip on the White House, as the country's voters responded positively to President Reagan's economic leadership and his foreign policy initiatives. His attack on rampant inflation was successful, notwithstanding the deep recession the country experienced in 1981–82. And he benefited politically from the big pickup in the economy that began in time for the 1984 election. Also, Reagan displayed sufficient toughness abroad, along with a shrewd concern for better relations with the Soviet Union, to conciliate various elements of the polity. As a result of those policies, coupled with his own increasing popularity, he accelerated the shift in voter allegiances from Democrat to Republican, especially in the South.

Yet the success of Reagan's policies came with a big price tag. His huge buildup of the military, along with deep tax cuts and the growing costs of various entitlement programs, increased the yearly federal deficit by many billions while adding trillions to the federal debt. In addition, the tax cuts he sponsored mostly benefited the people at the very top of the income and wealth scale, and further eroded the economic security of the middle class and the safety net of the working poor. So despite the fact that the Reagan economy produced eighteen million new jobs in the 1980s, wage stagnation remained a constant reality for a majority of working Americans.

Although Ronald Reagan departed the presidency in a blaze of glory, it was George Bush's misfortune that the recession of 1990–91 revealed that all was not well on the home front. (Federal Reserve Board

Chairman Alan Greenspan had acted too slowly to lower interest rates and to increase the money supply to counteract the downturn.) Although the economy did eventually begin to bounce back heading into the election year of 1992, over 7 percent of the workforce still remained unemployed. And that was bad news for Bush and good news for Democrats, especially for Bill Clinton.

As the state of the economy emerged as the chief focus of concern for politicians and voters alike, other Democratic candidates besides Clinton emerged to make a run at the nomination. They included Nebraska Senator Bob Kerrey, former Senator Paul Tsongas of Massachusetts, and Jerry Brown, one-time governor of California. Kerrey pushed a scheme for a national health insurance. Tsongas, a business-oriented Democrat, was a staunch advocate of deficit reduction. Brown endorsed a flat tax and embraced an agenda that also included the creation of new technologies to promote energy conservation.

With the advent of the primary season, Clinton successfully fought off charges of draft evasion and philandering and went on to earn a respectable second-place finish in the New Hampshire primary. Tsongas received 37 percent of the vote to his 25 percent. After celebrating his survival in New Hampshire as the "comeback kid," Clinton achieved important victories in many southern primaries on Super Tuesday (March 10), and consolidated his position as the front-runner. Following his triumph in such key primary states as Illinois and New York, Clinton put a lock on the Democratic nomination several months before the start of the scheduled July convention.

Clinton proved to be an agile and resourceful campaigner, supported by a good organization and ample funding. In addition, he broadened his appeal to many voters by calling for a middle-class tax cut and by supporting welfare reform and more cops on the beat. To demonstrate his toughness on crime, he even flew back to Little Rock during the New Hampshire primary to ensure that the execution of Ricky Ray Rector, a convicted murderer with an IQ of 64, would take place as scheduled. With this action, Clinton indicated that he was not going to be sideswiped in the manner that Michael Dukakis had been by George Bush in 1988 on the grounds that he was "soft on crime."

Notwithstanding Clinton's success in the Democratic primaries, he still had serious problems connecting with a majority of voters in his own party. They wanted someone other than Clinton to be the party's nominee, either because they did not like or trust him or because they weren't sure just where he stood on the issues. And his problems were not related just to his fellow Democrats. In the early summer, for example, he stood at only a little more than 20 percent in the national polls, with independent candidate Ross Perot, the Texas billionaire, and Republican incumbent George Bush running well ahead of him.

Clinton sought to reassure party doubters and independents across the spectrum. Thus, it was important for him not to be viewed as someone walking in Jesse Jackson's shadow. Consequently, while speaking to Jackson's Rainbow Coalition, he denounced the words of Sister Souljah, a black rap artist, who had suggested earlier that since blacks killed blacks every week, they might also take a week and kill whites. In addition, Clinton scored points with many big-city mayors by promising them a very large increase in federal aid to cope with their manifold urban problems. Thus, he proposed a series of expensive new government programs, amounting to nearly $220 billion over a four-year period, to help stimulate economic growth and employment in the private sector. With these initiatives he shored up his position within his own party. Polling data now showed that rank-and-file Democrats, hungry for victory in 1992, were not about to risk any further internal party division or conflict, which might spoil their chances to win in November.

Wanting harmony and cooperation, Democrats everywhere applauded Clinton's selection of Senator Al Gore of Tennessee as his running mate, a move he announced even before the start of the Democratic Convention in mid-July. Like Clinton, Gore was a fellow member of the DLC, who brought to the ticket a strong environmental commitment, a record of military service, and solid experience in Congress. The convention also responded positively to Clinton's cleverly crafted acceptance speech, in which he made a strong appeal to middle-class voters worried about their economic future and eager for change. In that context, Clinton had successfully projected himself as the agent of change and assured a national television audience that as president he would reach out with various programs to give assistance to those folks who played by the rules, paid their taxes, and raised their kids. At the same time, he insisted that the country's problems required solutions that were neither liberal nor conservative in character. In short, seeking to transcend the old categories, his goal was to reinvent government for the purpose of helping working people help themselves. But he also reaffirmed his commitment to a pro-choice agenda and promised to create eight million new jobs in four years, to reform health care, and "to end welfare as we know it."

While Clinton polished his acceptance speech, Ross Perot suddenly withdrew from the race in a move that took everyone by surprise. Perot, earlier, had surged to the front by lambasting Bush for his poor stewardship of the economy and by denouncing the prevailing gridlock in government as well as the huge federal deficits. But news about his authoritarian manner and his lack of specifics about how to deal with the various economic problems confronting the country had raised doubts about his candidacy among many voters. Clinton was the main beneficiary of Perot's departure, as it gave him the added momentum he needed to pull ahead of Bush in the polls.

Bush himself was already in deep trouble with conservatives in his own party. After pledging in 1988 to oppose all future tax hikes, he agreed to one in 1990 in order to avert a partial shutdown of the government. In addition, he reluctantly signed a civil rights bill, desired by many blue-ribbon corporations, that reaffirmed the principle of affirmative action, and, finally, he supported initiatives that enhanced the regulatory authority of the federal government.

Though they were unable to deny Bush the nomination, conservatives dominated the televised proceedings at the 1992 Republican Convention. Conservative pundit Patrick Buchanan, who had challenged Bush in the primaries, called for something akin to a declaration of war against the cultural left. Marilyn Quayle, the wife of Vice President Dan Quayle, attacked the so-called permissive generation of the 1960s, which, according to her, condoned draft evasion and the use of drugs. Thus, the defense of family values and a blanket opposition to a countercultural lifestyle had become the components of a GOP strategy to undermine Clinton's candidacy on the basis of his real or alleged character flaws.

By attacking Clinton with tactics that had worked for him in 1988, Bush ignored the economic fears of many middle-class Americans, largely because he had nothing to say to them. Yet they had good reason for concern: the unemployment rate had climbed to 7.6 percent in the late summer and early fall of 1992; thousands of jobs had been lost or had simply disappeared as a result of a deliberate corporate policy of downsizing the workforce; median household income had continued to decline since 1989; and medical costs climbed at a rapid rate.

Unlike Bush, who focused on Clinton's character, Clinton was guided by his campaign mantra, "It's the economy, stupid." Hence, he targeted job creation and economic growth as his number-one priority, which also included a pledge to stimulate investment in high-tech industries and the public infrastructure. But while Clinton was putting people first in his campaign literature, the federal deficit had jumped to a staggering $290 billion for fiscal year 1992. Faced with that stark figure, he also promised during the course of the campaign to reduce the federal deficit by half in four years. In addition, he endorsed the North American Free Trade Agreement (NAFTA), which President Bush had successfully negotiated with the leaders of Canada and Mexico, who agreed in principle to open their respective countries to a free flow of trade, goods, and services. Although the DLC and its corporate backers had fully embraced NAFTA, Clinton, aware of strong opposition coming from the ranks of organized labor and environmentalists, said that he would seek to negotiate stronger side agreements to protect their interests.

Clinton's endorsement of deficit reduction and NAFTA was not surprising. He was, after all, the candidate of the DLC, which strongly favored both issues and which had important connections on Wall Street. Indeed, some of Clinton's most significant campaign funding came from major investment houses, including Goldman Sachs, the longtime home of Robert Rubin, one of Clinton's important economic advisers. Also, many Silicon Valley firms, such as Apple Computer, were attracted to his proposal of government support for research and development in high-tech industries, as well as his free trade outlook and strong commitment to trade promotion. So they too provided him with ample financial help.

Although President Bush retained stronger business support than Clinton, his campaign for reelection was falling apart. He was hurt by Ross Perot's bizarre return to the campaign at the beginning of October. That Perot was back, and in good form, became clear in the three televised debates the candidates held during that final month of the campaign. Focusing on the deficit, economic stagnation, and gridlock, he reinforced Clinton's own case against Bush, which made it doubly difficult for the president to rebut criticism that came at him so effectively from both sides of the stage.

Thanks to the end of the Cold War, whose termination Bush had deftly managed, the 1992 campaign was fought almost entirely on the terrain of domestic politics and issues. Clinton did not ignore or slight questions of foreign policy. He attacked Bush's failure to emphasize human rights issues with regard to China; he denounced the administration's handling of Haitian refugees seeking entrance into the United States; he was highly critical of American policy in Bosnia for lacking firmness against the Serbian policy of ethnic cleansing; and he also insisted that the United States had a moral obligation to assume a leadership role in supporting and advancing the cause of global democracy.

Not surprisingly, Clinton's foreign policy remarks aroused little interest among voters. What mattered most to those suffering from the white-collar recession of 1990–91 was the current state of the American economy and deep concern about their future prospects. Although there had been a solid upturn in economic growth in 1992, particularly in the third and fourth quarters, the underlying reality was that too many Americans were still unemployed as a result of the recession of 1990–91, which spelled disaster for George Bush.

Clinton won the election with only 43 percent of the popular vote, but his margin of victory in the Electoral College was more substantial. He received 370 votes, carrying such strategically important states as California, New York, Ohio, and Illinois. He also enlarged the Democratic base in the South by winning Louisiana and Tennessee to go along with Arkansas and Georgia. On the other hand, his coattails were nonexistent, as the Democrats lost 10 seats in the House and gained none in the Senate. Furthermore, he himself ran well behind a majority of House Democrats elected in 1992. Yet Clinton probably helped many of those same Democrats by providing them with cover on matters such as crime and welfare reform.

George Bush's defeat, on the other hand, was massive. From having won nearly 54 percent of the popular vote in 1988, his total was reduced to 38 percent in 1992. Despite having carried both Texas and Florida, he won only 170 votes in the Electoral College. Bush's failure to reassure voters that he cared about their problems and that he understood their concerns, at a time of ruthless corporate downsizing, was enough to kill his reelection bid. His defeat appeared to mark the end of the Reagan era in American politics.

Ross Perot won 19 percent of the vote but carried no states. Yet his impact on the outcome of the election was significant. He became a lightning rod for considerable voter discontent with government, particularly on matters such as the size of the federal deficit and gridlock. Earlier, his withdrawal from the contest in July had propelled Clinton to the front. His return in October helped to focus voter attention on economic issues, which was the strength of Clinton's campaign against Bush. Aware of Perot's impact on the issues, Democratic Senator Daniel Patrick Moynihan remarked, in the immediate aftermath of an election that gave the Democrats control of the White House and Congress for the first time since 1980, "My God . . . now it's *our* deficit."

With the 1992 election, Bill Clinton had finally realized his dream of moving from Little Rock to Washington and becoming president. By any estimation, it was a stunning achievement, especially in light of the difficulties he had encountered at the beginning of the primary season over questions about his private behavior. Clinton had triumphed in part by running as a Washington outsider on one hand and a centrist on social issues on the other. He was no 1960s liberal in disguise: his desire to reform the New Deal welfare system and his support of the death penalty made that clear. On the other hand, like a good 1990s progressive, he spoke in favor of feminist causes and gay rights. Yet he recognized that the key to his election success was the economy. With the help of his good friend Harvard Professor Robert Reich, he had offered a program that recognized the need to use government to repair the damage to public institutions resulting from the Reagan revolution. But Clinton sent the voters a mixed message—on one hand, he supported major funding for job training and public investments, while on the other he embraced the cause of deficit reduction. That contradiction was self-evident, and it represented the divided soul and dual character of President-elect Bill Clinton's incoming administration.

LIBRARY
THE UNIVERSITY OF TEXAS
AT BROWNSVILLE
Brownsville, Tx 78520-4991

Chapter Two

From Winning to Losing

During the interim period between the general election of 1992 and the transfer of political power on January 20, 1993, Bill Clinton organized his administration, appointed members of his Cabinet, and prepared an agenda for his first year in office. Most of that business took place in Little Rock, where he selected Warren Christopher, a former Carter administration official, as secretary of state. Les Aspin, chair of the House Armed Services Committee, became secretary of defense; Lloyd Bentsen, conservative Democratic senator from Texas, secretary of treasury; Ron Brown, chair of the Democratic National Committee, secretary of commerce; and Robert Reich, professor at the Kennedy School of Government, secretary of labor. Responding to the desire of women voters who had supported him in 1992, he appointed Donna Shalala, chancellor at the University of Wisconsin, to head the Department of Human Services, and Hazel O'Leary, a corporate executive, took over the Department of Energy. Altogether, it was a Cabinet that the *Wall Street Journal* aptly described as "a new elite, people who studied at the best universities, who largely escaped the war of their generation and, in many cases, who struck it rich in the decade they now often criticize."

Other appointees included Congressman Leon Panetta as budget director, lawyer Mickey Kantor as trade negotiator, and Wall Street mogul Robert Rubin as chair of the National Economic Council. Thomas McLarty, a close childhood friend of Clinton and a well-placed Arkansas businessman, became White House chief of staff. George Stephanopoulos, a key campaign strategist and policy adviser, assumed similar duties in the new administration. Most important, Vice President Al Gore and Hillary Clinton, the first lady, functioned as consultants and confidants to the new president, with the authority to advise him on a complete range of policy matters if they so chose.

While Clinton addressed staffing problems, the matter of the budget deficit began to weigh on him. When he met with Alan Greenspan, chairman of the Federal Reserve Board, in Little Rock shortly after the election, Greenspan emphasized the need to bring the rising federal deficit under control in order to prevent a return of inflation and to free up funds for investment in the private sector. In addition, it would have the positive effect of lowering interest rates in the bond market, which, he believed, would produce strong and steady economic growth in the near term.

What was the bond market and why did Greenspan place such a heavy emphasis on it? According to Louis Uchitelle, a business reporter for the *New York Times*, "the American economy is governed by the bond market—a loose confederation of wealthy Americans, bankers, financiers, money managers, rich foreigners, executives of life insurance companies, presidents of universities and nonprofit foundations, pensioners and people who once kept their money in passbooks savings accounts (or under the bed) and now buy shares in mutual funds." In other words, the $10 trillion that bondholders had put into the economy by 1994, on which interest would have to be paid, constituted a form of economic power that intimidated almost everybody, including the president of the United States. So if Clinton heeded the call for deficit reduction to satisfy the bond market, he hoped that it would encourage Greenspan to pursue a flexible monetary policy on behalf of noninflationary growth. For Greenspan, that meant restraining even the slightest burst of inflation because, reported the *New York Times*, "bondholders . . . often fear that a tight labor market and robust growth will lead to higher inflation."

That the markets were looking for a proper cue from the chief executive was a point that both Clinton and Greenspan well understood. At the same time, important political and economic elites, including a bipartisan majority in Congress, leading business organizations, and most mainstream economists, were also demanding action, which put added pressure on Clinton to move in that direction. Nor could he ignore the fact that Ross Perot had won 19 percent of the popular vote after making deficit reduction and the goal of a balanced budget central to his campaign.

On the other hand, most Americans wanted the new president to take immediate action to spur the economy and to lower unemployment. For them deficit reduction ranked near the bottom of their concerns, which is why Clinton did not focus on the issue to any great extent during the campaign. Hence, he simply concentrated on the need for jobs and new public investments to go along with welfare and health care reform. Yet by the time he took office, the deficit hawks inside the new administration were winning the debate to shape the administration's major priorities.

Lined up on one side were Treasury Secretary Lloyd Bentsen, Robert Rubin and Leon Panetta, who favored a financial-markets strategy. On the other were Labor Secretary Robert Reich and campaign consultants James Carville and Stanley Greenberg, who were committed to a substantial public investment strategy and the keeping of campaign promises. Meanwhile, awaiting the outcome of this debate was Alan Greenspan, who earlier had cautioned Clinton about the need to engage in a program of serious deficit reduction.

While his advisers debated, Bill Clinton was sworn in as the 42nd president of the United States. Giving a spirited inaugural address, he sought to project himself as the agent of change who would seek to restore the people's confidence in government and public institutions. Clinton promised "to force the spring" of an "American renewal." Moving quickly to counter past Republican policies, he issued an executive order ending the federal prohibition on the use of fetal tissue for medical research, and he authorized the use of federal funds to provide abortion counseling in federally funded health clinics. On February 4, 1993, Clinton also signed a family leave bill, twice vetoed by George Bush, that guaranteed workers up to twelve weeks per year of unpaid leave for medical emergencies.

But notwithstanding Clinton's best intentions to get off to a fast start in the spirit of Franklin Roosevelt's first one hundred days, he was quickly entangled in a mess that was indicative of things to come. Pressured by women's groups to appoint a woman to a major Cabinet post, he selected Zoe Baird, a corporate lawyer, for the position of attorney general. Unfortunately for all concerned, she quickly became embroiled in controversy, having earlier hired an illegal nanny for whom she had neglected to pay Social Security taxes. Once this became public knowledge, Baird's nomination engendered opposition, and she withdrew her name from consideration. Eventually, Clinton settled on Janet Reno, a Florida prosecutor, who was quickly approved by the Senate as attorney general.

Also embarrassing to Clinton was the brouhaha that erupted over his nomination of Lani Guinier to head the Justice Department's Civil Rights Division. A close friend of both Bill and Hillary Clinton from their days at Yale Law School, she seemed well qualified for the position. But after her various academic publications on civil rights were carefully scrutinized, it appeared that she had endorsed a theory of proportional representation for minority candidates in legislative elections rather than accepting the traditional win-lose result based on a majority of votes. Her position precipitated a major row among various interest groups inside the Democratic Party, and it immediately led to big trouble for Clinton in the Senate. Having little stomach for pushing Guinier through an uncertain confirmation process, Clinton, mindful of the growing opposition to her, pulled the nomination, producing intense outrage among her many black and white supporters.

Far more damaging to the president was the fight over gay rights. During the 1992 campaign, Clinton had pledged to support gay rights by opposing discrimination in the military. But while some in the gay movement welcomed his commitment, others wanted him to endorse as his first priority legislation promoting fair and equal opportunity and employment for gays in the workplace. Instead, he announced on January 28, 1993, a policy of ending discrimination against gays in the armed forces, which quickly produced a wave of opposition in Congress and the Defense Department.

Key senators, led by Sam Nunn, chairman of the Senate Armed Services Committee, and General Colin Powell, chairman of the Joint Chiefs, weighed in against the proposed change. Frustrated by such strong resistance to his proposal, Clinton finally was forced to accept a compromise based on the principle of "don't ask, don't tell." Gays were understandably disappointed with that outcome, and some felt that Clinton had sold out. But, in the meantime, he had paid a stiff political price for taking his stand. Poll data confirmed that since Clinton took office, his public image as a moderate Democrat had slipped dramatically. Many more people now viewed him as another liberal who governed from the cultural left, not from the New Democratic center from which he had ostensibly campaigned in 1992.

Clinton's conflict with the military chiefs over the issue of gays in the military marked the beginning of a strained relationship. They questioned his priorities and leadership ability, and he was decidedly uncomfortable with their military culture. In time, however, Clinton's dealings with the brass improved, but administration officials later admitted that because he was "unwilling to exercise full authority over military commanders," civilian control over the military establishment "eroded" during his presidency.

The confrontation at Waco, Texas, between the government and cult leader David Koresh and his followers, ensconced in their compound, added to Clinton's difficulties in the spring of 1993. After a fire engulfed the structure, killing Koresh and those who remained with him, some people wondered whether the government's tactics might have produced this tragic outcome. The administration also faced questions as to who actually authorized and assumed responsibility for the government's action at Waco, President Clinton or Attorney General Janet Reno. That appearance of the administration's disorganization, stemming from the Waco tragedy, hurt Clinton at a time when he was still trying to gain his political footing in Washington.

Yet Clinton knew that the state of the economy would determine his fate as president. He sought to focus on the economy "like a laser beam," but quickly discovered that governing was not the same as campaigning, that promises made during the heat of a campaign were often impossible to keep, and that choices between conflicting demands were difficult to reconcile. Clinton had based his political career in Arkansas on his ability to synthesize precisely such opposites in order to find common ground among the contesting parties. His coping with a complex budget process in Washington would soon test that skill, faced as he was with two dramatically different views on how best to define the administration's economic priorities.

Because Clinton faced severe institutional pressure from market forces, along with demands for deficit reduction emerging from major business organizations and Congress, he had little room in which to maneuver. When he and his advisers finally settled on a package that they had worked out after considerable discussion and debate, he not only decreased the scope of his public investments program but also rescinded his promised middle-class tax cut. Still, the program he presented to Congress in mid-February 1993 contained some striking features. It included a commitment to deficit reduction, higher taxes on wealthy citizens, a hike in corporate taxes, an energy tax to help pay for a modified public investment program, cuts in the military budget, a proposal for a short-term economic stimulus, and a tax credit for the working poor.

More specifically, Clinton's plan called for a projected deficit cut of nearly $500 billion over a five-year period, which would be divided almost evenly between spending cuts and tax increases. It also stipulated a marginal tax rate of 36 percent on Americans earning $115,000 a year and a top rate of 39.6 percent on affluent Americans making at least $250,000 a year. The military budget was lowered by $112 billion over a five-year period, and various entitlements were cut by $144 billion for the same period. At the same time, a wide-ranging new tax tied to energy use would provide funds necessary to underwrite Clinton's various public investment initiatives, including a stimulus measure of $16.3 billion to promote job creation.

Clinton's program amounted to what Greenspan had encouraged, so the Federal Reserve Board chairman publicly endorsed it. At the same time, interest rates on long-term bonds began to decline, much to the satisfaction of the White House. In addition, poll data confirmed that a majority of Americans supported Clinton's program, as did executives of various corporations who met at the White House just a few days after Clinton delivered his message to Congress.

Clinton's plan, however, soon encountered strong opposition from elements in the business community. Although virtually all interest groups favored deficit reduction as their sine qua non, many older manufacturing firms took a stand against the proposed energy tax and the requested increase in corporate taxes. The head of Aluminum Corporation of America, for example, suggested that a gasoline tax replace the energy tax, claiming that without such a change plants would have to close or be forced to leave the United States in order to remain competitive. Meanwhile, many in the banking and financial community intimated that they could live with an energy tax if funds gathered from that tax were used for deficit reduction. But those heavily dependent on gasoline such as truckers and agribusiness flatly opposed any such increase in gasoline taxes. As a result of those divergent interests, multiple and conflicting pressures from business were soon felt in Congress.

While business opposition to parts of his plan grew, Clinton had to cope with a Democratic Congress also intent on advancing the cause of deficit reduction. Congress, in a nonbinding budget resolution, retained spending caps that effectively limited spending on new or current domestic programs unless monies for such programs came from agreed cuts in other existing programs. This action ensured that Clinton's budget would be left with less than $1 billion for new investments in 1994 and less than $6 billion in 1995. Outraged by this situation, he reportedly asked staff members, "Where are the Democrats? We are all Eisenhower Republicans here and we are fighting Reagan Republicans. We stand for lower deficits and free trade and the bond market. Isn't that great?"

In the meantime, as a result of a successful Republican filibuster, the Senate blocked the passage of the administration's emergency stimulus package of $16 billion, which was designed to promote summer jobs and to extend a $2.5 billion block grant to the cities. Its failure was another indication of the deepening problems Clinton now faced with his entire budget. Not only did he lack Republican support on this issue but he now faced a powerful coalition of large and small business organizations, which had launched a well-financed grassroots mobilization to oppose his energy tax. Business had apparently found a vulnerable chink in Clinton's armor by claiming that jobs would be lost as a result of this tax and that it was akin to a middle-class tax hike.

While debate swirled, the House finally passed a budget bill without one Republican vote of support. As Clinton's package went over to the Senate, the energy tax faced a concerted attack from business interests and conservative Democrats alike. Unfortunately for Clinton, it was excised from the legislation, which meant that funds designed to finance key investment programs were no longer available. A 4.3-cent increase per gallon in the gasoline tax, having replaced the energy tax, effectively reduced the projected revenue intake from $71 billion to only $24.2 billion over a five-year period. That legislative change forced a scaling back of monies allotted for programs such as the Earned Income Tax Credit for the working poor.

The final congressional budget package included a commitment to a nearly $500 billion reduction in the federal deficit over a five-year period, which was predicated on a nearly $250 billion in deficit reduction and roughly $250 billion in new tax revenues. It also provided for a 36 percent marginal tax rate on incomes over $115,000, a top rate of

39.6 percent on incomes over $250,000, and a 1 percent increase in the highest corporate tax rate. In addition, an earned income tax credit was extended to families of the working poor, and the gasoline tax was hiked to 4.3 cents a gallon. Finally, spending was trimmed back somewhat on several entitlement programs, including Medicare.

Despite considerable changes in the original Clinton package, the passage of this legislation was in doubt in each chamber until the very last vote had been counted. Losing every Republican vote and some Democratic votes, the administration, in early August 1993, squeaked through the House with a 218–216 victory, and Vice President Gore had to break a 50–50 vote in the Senate to ensure final passage of the administration's first budget. At the same time, much of what Clinton had requested in the way of an investment strategy, or a jobs program, lay in tatters on the floor of each chamber as a result of spending caps and business pressure to remove the energy tax.

As a result of that action, Clinton's public investments agenda had been reduced to "symbolic dimensions," and he was now dependent on the private sector to generate economic growth sufficient to produce an upturn in employment and middle-class job security. But despite the fact that Clinton's tax increase affected only the upper 3 percent of taxpayers, with the major burden falling on the top 1 percent of all filers, the Republicans, who stood united in their opposition to him, claimed that he had raised taxes on the middle class. That GOP charge would eventually come back to haunt Clinton and many congressional Democrats during the 1994 midterm election.

Clinton embarked on the most controversial move of his first year in office long before the budget battle of 1993 was finally resolved. Within five days of having become president, he appointed Hillary Clinton to head a task force that would recommend a program of action to reform the American health industry, which accounted for over 14 percent of the gross domestic product. Mrs. Clinton moved quickly to put the wheels in motion and selected Ira Magaziner, an experienced policy innovator, to organize and manage her study group. Work began on a reform package to restructure an industry that had left thirty-seven million Americans without any health insurance or coverage at a time when accelerating costs to business and individuals alike had created what appeared to be a major health care crisis in America.

Yet others disagreed. Senator Moynihan downplayed the notion of a health care crisis and argued that a majority of Americans were still effectively covered by some kind of insurance. Moynihan preferred that Clinton first deal with a "crisis" in welfare, leaving aside the other for what he considered to be more urgent business requiring the president's full attention. But Clinton was not deterred. Prospective action on welfare reform was shelved for future consideration.

The Clinton task force quickly moved its discussion and consultations behind closed doors, while adopting a framework and agenda to deal with the host of complicated issues needing careful analysis, such as how to extend coverage and contain costs. It quickly rejected a single-payer model that had worked well in Canada, a model that provided universal coverage as well as freedom of choice and that-was paid for out of general tax revenues. Instead, the task force was guided by an approach already taken by the Jackson Hole Group, which included representatives and sponsors from major insurance companies, hospital and physician bodies, as well as other powerful elements inside the American medical industry. This group had already examined ways of containing the escalating costs of the medical industry to American business, and it was also intent on preventing any threat to its privileged position coming from increased government regulation. Not surprisingly, its prescription emphasized the centrality of market forces, tied to the creation of health maintenance organizations (HMOs), as the proper modality for limiting corporate and business costs.

Using that recommendation as its template, the Clinton task force—contrary to the wishes of the Jackson Hole Group—also adopted a regulatory system of sorts that gave the federal government an enhanced role in shaping the future structure of the medical industry. Although key officials from the Treasury Department felt that its plan of action lacked a proper internal review process and was built on a foundation of illusions with respect to price controls, the White House, eager to present a bill, disregarded all such internal criticism. Upon receiving his task force's 240,000-word report, Clinton went to Congress on September 22, 1993, and called for prompt action on what he called "our most urgent priority."

The cornerstone of Clinton's Health Security Act, wrote journalist Jacob Hacker, was "universal health insurance through competing private health plans. Under managed competition most Americans would obtain health insurance through new regional insurance purchasing cooperatives that would contract with private health plans and monitor the competition among them." Costs were to be contained by capping health insurance premiums, by placing limits on Medicare, and by implementing a successful operation of managed competition. Clinton also proposed to increase tobacco taxes to fund the projected $100 billion needed to start the program.

The public at first welcomed the Clinton plan, though few Americans understood how it worked. Its complexity baffled them. Many large businesses, associated with the Business Roundtable, were initially positive in their response and saw it as an opportunity to reduce their labor costs. Opposition soon began to grow both in and out of Congress. Al From, president of the DLC, feared that "The Administration's plan has many of the earmarks of a new entitlement program." More significantly, the Business Roundtable, which had failed to endorse the Clinton bill, now supported the more moderate Cooper–Breaux bill because "it was built around market mechanisms rather than mandates." Small businesses rebelled at the prospect of having to pay a mandated 80 percent of their employees' health benefits. In addition, small and medium insurance companies went on the attack, fearing that they would be the losers if the administration's bill, benefiting large insurance companies, was passed by Congress. Eventually, these attacks began to take their toll, as more and more Americans felt less inclined to change the current fee-for-service system, especially now that there had been an upturn in the economy in early and mid-1994 and a downturn in the inflation rate of health insurance.

So when Congress finally began to consider health care legislation in early 1994, it was subject to intense interest group pressure from all sides. Members of both chambers soon divided into a number of factions, supporting proposals running from single-payer to all-out opposition to any change in the current system. On the other hand, Senate Minority Leader Bob Dole was initially disposed to compromise their differences. The White House refused to weaken the provision for universal coverage and thereby lost whatever opportunity it had to attract significant Republican support to pass some kind of bill.

Although Clinton lost the battle over health care legislation, he prevailed in the struggle to pass the Brady Bill, which was named after

President Ronald Reagan's press secretary, who was paralyzed by gunfire during an attempted assassination of Reagan. It passed the Congress in November 1993 and legislated a five-day waiting period for anyone seeking to purchase a handgun.

Far more important was the struggle to ratify the North American Free Trade Agreement (NAFTA), which had been a Bush administration project designed to link Canada, Mexico, and the United States into a unified free-market trading zone. During the 1992 campaign, Clinton endorsed NAFTA but asserted that stronger side agreements were needed to protect labor and environmental concerns. Once in office, however, he embraced the treaty and went along with a congressional fast-track arrangement that required an up-or-down vote on it without amendments.

NAFTA was an especially divisive issue within the Democratic Party. The proposed treaty was strongly opposed by organized labor and environmental groups. They feared that their basic interests and concerns had not been adequately addressed by the treaty Bush had signed in December 1992. Labor worried about likely job losses to Mexico, and the Sierra Club, among many other environmental organizations, thought that the treaty would do little to head off the spread of pollution and contamination originating from Mexican sources into the United States. On the other hand, corporate America and politicians from both parties, including House Republican Whip Newt Gingrich, worked in tandem with the White House to promote its passage. After Vice President Al Gore had made a strong case for ratification in a televised debate with Ross Perot on *Larry King Live*, a majority in favor of the treaty solidified in the House. Despite opposition to it from many House Democrats, led by Majority Leader Richard Gephardt, the treaty cleared the House, without binding labor or environmental guarantees or meaningful side agreements. It encountered little resistance in the Senate and thus became law, much to the satisfaction of the White House, the Business Roundtable, and powerful political and corporate interests in Mexico and Canada.

Looking back at NAFTA several years later, it seems that organized labor had good reason to worry about job losses and that the concerns of various environmental groups were not misplaced. Although the migration of jobs to Mexico never reached the numbers the leadership of the AFL-CIO had feared, there were still significant losses as companies such as General Motors moved production south of the border, operating many plants on Mexican soil. In addition, many other companies threatened to move to Mexico as a way of intimidating workers who were participating in union organizing drives. In short, NAFTA had become a useful club in management's hands in an attempt to subdue an American workforce hoping to negotiate better working conditions for itself.

At the same time, the media reported that weak pollution controls on the Mexican side of the border were wreaking havoc on the environmental landscape of Texas and other states bordering on Mexico. Thus, the failure of the Clinton administration to allay labor and environmental concerns would lead to a growing opposition to its later efforts to negotiate other fast-track arrangements designed to expand NAFTA.

For the Clinton administration, the fight to ratify NAFTA, along with its approval of a newly renewed GATT treaty (General Agreement on Tariffs and Trade), revealed a key element of its global economic strategy, which was at the core of its foreign policy. Clinton was determined to increase American shares in the global marketplace, a point he made often while speaking to business executives during the 1992 campaign. As he remarked after becoming president:

> The truth of our age is this and must be this: open and competitive commerce will enrich us as a nation. It spurs us to innovate. It forces us to compete, it connects us with new customers. It promotes global growth without which no rich country can hope to grow wealthy. . . . And I say to you in the face of all the pressures to do the reverse, we must compete, not retreat.

While Clinton served as governor of Arkansas, he had participated in twelve overseas trade missions to both Europe and Asia, and he appreciated their value. So when Secretary of Commerce Ron Brown and Trade Representative Mickey Kantor went abroad to open doors for Boeing and General Motors and other American multinational business interests, they spoke for a president who staked American domestic prosperity and growth on exports, which were greatly accelerated and coordinated by his administration. Thanks to that degree of commitment from the White House, American ambassadors had become, in the words of *Business Week*, "unabashed peddlers in pinstripes, vigorously lobbying local officials on behalf of Corporate America."

Yet despite Clinton's insistence on making and keeping the United States the world leader inside the global economy, not everyone at home did do well as result of that subsequent export surge. Although unemployment had declined slightly at the end of 1993, wage stagnation was still a harsh reality for a majority of working Americans. Median family income had dropped from $38,129 in 1991 to $36,953 in 1993. In fact, in the years from 1989 to 1993 the average American family had lost $2,344 in annual income, which represented a decline of 7 percent. More people now lived in poverty than at any time since the Reagan years. While the top 20 percent of the workforce received 48 percent of all earned income, the bottom fifth took home only 3.6 percent. One percent of households in 1992 controlled nearly 40 percent of the country's wealth, including 49.5 percent of stocks, while the top 10 percent held 85.2 percent of stocks and 91.3 percent of all bonds. (In contrast with these figures, the bottom 40 percent of households controlled 0.2 percent of the nation's wealth.)

The Clinton administration confronted the problem of the increasingly vast inequality in income and wealth distribution by introducing an element of progressivity into the tax structure. Building on the Reagan administration's program, it also sought to help families of the working poor by expanding the earned income tax credit, which by 1998 allowed people making between $10,200 and $30,580 per year to receive an average annual payment of $1,890 a year. But aside from these changes, it had little to offer those Americans suffering from the rapid and radical changes taking place in the workforce and labor markets as a result of massive corporate downsizing. Many tens of thousands of workers faced the likely prospect of losing their jobs, or had been already removed from the work rolls, as corporations such as General Motors, IBM, ATT, and Xerox sought to cut costs and to improve productivity through computerization and robotization of the work process. Consequently, owners of "capital assets," such as plants and machinery, and a "technological aristocracy," promoting the reengineering of work, primarily benefited from the rapid downsizing occurring at the expense of workers on assembly lines and elsewhere in the private sector.

Unlike the deep recession of 1981–82, which saw mostly blue-collar workers losing jobs, a good many of those workers displaced during the early 1990s came from the ranks of middle management, including the white-collar workforce of the service sector. Clearly, those economic anxieties that had driven them to support Clinton in 1992 had not yet abated. Despite the administration's accurate claim that two million new jobs had been created, many workers still worried about their future job prospects resulting from the vagaries of the marketplace both in a domestic and in a global context.

Among Clinton's Cabinet officers, Secretary of Labor Robert Reich was singularly concerned about corporate downsizing. Hence, he spoke often about the need to upgrade the skills of workers so that they would be in a better position to compete for new jobs, many computer related, which were indeed becoming available as a result of the great shifts in the technological aspects of work. He recognized that the problem of a rapidly growing wage inequality was caused not just by downturns in the business cycle but by changes in the nature of work inside the system itself.

The near collapse of the American labor movement contributed to the persistent wage inequality. Because the sclerotic leadership of the AFL-CIO lacked the capacity to recruit new workers or to successfully mount serious strikes to defend worker rights and to gain higher wages, it was in deep trouble. Furthermore, the fact that only 14.5 percent of the 129 million Americans at work were union members underscored its radically weakened position vis-à-vis corporate America. Thus, having already lost the battle to a New Democratic president over the ratification of NAFTA, labor was in political and economic limbo, with no strategy or program to cope with corporate downsizing, globalization, and widespread public hostility. Unlike the Great Society of the Lyndon Johnson era, millions of Americans, from the cultural left to the corporate right, now viewed organized labor as a fossil from a bygone era.

As labor struggled to find its voice, Clinton had his own problems. Although he and the Democratic majority in Congress had worked well enough together to pass a budget, a family leave bill, motor voter registration, and the Brady Bill, his victory on the budget had been razor-thin and lacked any Republican support. His legislative triumph on NAFTA had alienated labor and liberal Democrats in the House. Many more voters now viewed him with distrust as a result of recent revelations about a possible shady land deal in Arkansas back in the 1980s, and his initial support of gay rights in the military had incurred the hostility, if not hatred, of virtually all conservative voters.

More serious health care legislation, which was the key component of Clinton's domestic agenda, was ground to bits in the legislative mill after strong opposition developed in Congress and across the country. By the late summer of 1994, the congressional Democratic leadership, knowing that the bill would not pass, refused even to bring it to the floor of either chamber for an up-or-down vote. Ironically, Clinton's Health Security Act, having been introduced with such great fanfare back in September 1993, had now become a millstone around the neck of the Democratic Party, much to the delight of House Minority Whip Newt Gingrich, who led the opposition to it. Two years later, in the summer of 1996, a wiser and much chastened Bill Clinton admitted, "I overestimated the extent to which a person elected with a minority of votes in an environment that was complex, to say the least, could achieve a sweeping overhaul of the health care system when no previous president had been able to do it for decades and decades."

Clinton's traumatic defeat over health care gave the GOP a powerful issue with which to attack the administration on the eve of the 1994 midterm election. But Clinton's problems, stemming from a land deal in Arkansas known as Whitewater, along with a charge of a sexual impropriety by a former Arkansas state employee, had already put a cloud over his administration that would cause him grief for years to come. The Whitewater controversy, erupting publicly in 1993, brought into focus the business activities of both Bill and Hillary Clinton during their Arkansas years. It involved their joint partnership in an unprofitable real estate investment in northwest Arkansas with James McDougal. But complicating matters for the Clintons was the fact that McDougal was also chief proprietor of the Madison Guaranty Savings and Loan of Little Rock, which had crashed during the savings and loan debacle of the 1980s. After federal regulators examined Madison's books in the aftermath of its collapse (which cost the federal government over $70 million to bail out), questions arose as to whether McDougal had siphoned money from the bank to buttress the failing Whitewater land scheme, and whether he had also illegally diverted funds from the bank to help pay for Clinton's 1984 reelection campaign for governor.

During that period, Hillary Clinton, a partner at Rose Law Firm of Little Rock, had served as the bank's legal representative, which posed a possible conflict of interest between herself and the state regulator of the banking business appointed by her husband. Her role as the bank's legal representative also caught the attention of federal regulators examining the causes for the bank's demise. Following their investigation, they sent referrals to officials in the Treasury and Justice Departments that included the names of both Clintons, though this did not necessarily mean that either had been involved in criminal or wrongful activity. At some point, however, that privileged information was leaked to the White House as a result of improper briefings given to members of the White House staff by other government officials.

After public controversy erupted, which cast a ray of doubt and suspicion on the honesty and trustworthiness of the first couple, President Clinton, under considerable pressure to clear the air, agreed to the appointment of an independent counsel to investigate the matter. Hence, Attorney General Janet Reno selected former federal prosecutor Robert Fiske Jr. to examine the business activities of the Clintons in the 1980s, including the first lady's work as legal counsel at Madison, and to investigate the death of White House Deputy Counsel Vincent Foster in July 1993, whose White House files may have included a set of Mrs. Clinton's billing records for Madison. (Several years later, when those billing records were finally uncovered, they undercut her claim that her work for Madison had been of only a minimal nature.)

Congress's investigation of the Whitewater affair led to the resignation of several officials in the Treasury Department, adding to the growing suspicion about the trustworthiness of the Clintons. Nevertheless, no solid evidence was adduced to implicate either the president or the first lady in wrongdoing. Fiske helped matters by submitting a report that also exculpated administration officials from any criminal mischief on matters bearing on Whitewater. And he further affirmed that Foster had not been murdered, as rumored by some conspiracy mongers on the political right, but died as a result of suicide.

But the potential for serious trouble remained after Congress renewed the Independent Counsel Act, which Clinton signed in June 1994. Little did he know that his signing of this legislation would carry with it far-reaching consequences for his presidency. Several months later, a three-judge federal panel appointed Kenneth Starr, a respected Washington lawyer who had served as solicitor general in the Bush administration, to replace Fiske and to continue the investigation of the administration. Whether Starr would find anything new or different from what was already contained in the Fiske report depended on factors beyond Bill Clinton's control.

The brouhaha over Whitewater completely overshadowed another troubling piece of news for Clinton, which would also have major long-term implications for the fate of his presidency. It began with a published article in the *American Spectator* asserting that Arkansas state troopers had procured women for him, including someone named Paula. On February 11, 1994, Paula Corbin Jones announced at a press conference in Washington that she was the Paula mentioned in the article, but she insisted that Clinton's sexual entreaties had been rejected during her brief visit to his hotel room in Little Rock on May 8, 1991. Although Clinton later said that he did not recall meeting her, she demanded an apology from him. Because he did not give it, she moved to clear her name by filing a suit for damages, amounting to $700,000, in a federal district court in Little Rock on May 6, 1994, against both Clinton and the state trooper who had brought her to the governor's hotel room for a sexual liaison. Subsequently, the president's attorneys sought to postpone legal action on the case until he left office, but the American Civil Liberties Union, joining conservative groups supporting Jones, asked that court action be not deferred. In the meantime, Federal Judge Susan Webber Wright ruled that although the trial could be postponed, pretrial questioning could still be undertaken.

While the Jones case was being litigated, Clinton had business to transact in the area of foreign policy. Having taken office with the intention of focusing on domestic matters, he was quickly drawn into the foreign policy arena, as unresolved problems from the Bush administration spilled over into his own. Thus, Clinton had no alternative but to confront a series of difficult issues that had little or nothing to do with finding export markets for American goods and investment capital. Most reluctantly, he had to deal with the presence of American troops in Somalia, a flood of refugees from Haiti, a murderous ethnic war in Bosnia, conflict in the Middle East, trade relations with Japan, human rights issues in China, and complex negotiations with Russia in the aftermath of the Cold War. When faced with such pressing problems just barely into his presidency, he understandably complained that "foreign policy is not what I came here to do."

Clinton's primary objective was to enlarge the scope of democracy and to extend free markets in a global setting, while hoping that they would serve to advance both economic and strategic interests for the United States. But if the goal of enlarging "the world's free community of market democracies" provided something of an ideological grounding for an American foreign policy in need of a new function and role in the post–Cold War world, Clinton soon found out that events themselves often drove policy.

American involvement in Somalia, for example, affected Clinton's foreign policy in a profound way. By adding more troops to those George Bush had already dispatched to this poor East African country to help in the distribution of food supplies sent to cope with widespread famine, he quickly found himself at war with rival gangs contesting for control in the country's capital. After a number of American troops were killed in a botched raid in search of a key gang leader, Clinton was under enormous domestic pressure to remove those troops from the scene, which he later did. That experience not only undermined his willingness to employ force ostensibly not under direct American control, but it reinforced his hesitation and reservation about using troops anywhere on the globe where vital American interests were not directly involved.

Although domestic political pressure led Clinton to withdraw troops from Somalia, it also helps to explain why he was prepared to send troops to Haiti in 1994. While a fresh flood of Cuban refugees had been allowed to land in Florida in the late summer of 1994, Haitian refugees, also seeking shelter in Florida, were quarantined elsewhere in the Caribbean. Although Clinton earlier had been critical of Bush's handling of the Haitian refugee problem, claiming that it had not been humane in practice, he now felt the need to stem the tide coming from Haiti to Florida, or face intense criticism in the Sunshine State and risk losing Democratic seats in Congress in 1994 and the state to a Republican challenger in 1996.

Clinton hoped to give Haitians a stake at home, so he sent troops to restore its democratically elected president, removed in a coup, to his former position of authority. Despite strong opposition in Congress to this move, Clinton's policy worked on two levels: it stemmed the flow northward, and he retained the loyalty of the Congressional Black Caucus by symbolically restoring an element of democracy in the most destitute and poverty-ridden country of the Americas.

Bosnia was a far more difficult nut for President Clinton to crack. He had no solution there short of sending American troops to help end the fighting in a war that had produce the horrible spectacle of ethnic cleansing. But Clinton feared putting American troops in harm's way and would not dispatch any into the war zone. So once again, as in the case of Haiti, his sharp campaign criticism of Bush's foreign policy in Bosnia was contradicted in practice now that he was in the White House facing the same bleak options that earlier had confronted his predecessor.

Clinton did score a major symbolic triumph by bringing Yitzhak Rabin, the prime minister of Israel, and Yasser Arafat, the leader of the Palestine Liberation Organization, to the White House in August 1994. There, they signed an agreement that created the legal basis for Palestinian home rule in Gaza and elsewhere on the West Bank. Although that partial reconciliation between the two adversaries had been inspired by secret diplomacy undertaken by their representatives in Oslo, Norway, Clinton had played an important role by encouraging the continuation of talks so as to keep the peace process moving along the right track.

Japan posed an entirely different problem for the Clinton administration. Having already built a huge trade surplus with the United States, Japan now refused to open its home markets to the importation of American cellular phones, which it had agreed to in 1989. Hence, President Clinton, working through his trade negotiator, Mickey Kantor, was prepared to foster a showdown with Tokyo. Japan, now under considerable American pressure to open its doors to a variety of American goods, reached several trade agreements with Washington in October 1994 and early 1995, which averted the likely imposition of trade sanctions by the United States.

America's relations with China were even more complicated and fraught with the possibility of a deepening crisis. During the 1992 campaign, Clinton had attacked George Bush's failure to emphasize the importance of human rights in his dealings with Beijing. However intent Clinton may have been in making policy on that basis, he soon discovered that a human rights agenda vis-à-vis China would stand in the way of progress in other areas, including the forging of Sino-American trade agreements and the obtaining of China's cooperation in halting the dispersal of nuclear technology to countries such as Iran.

Despite Clinton's forgoing his threat to remove most-favored-nation status for China unless it improved its human rights position, the two sides sharply disagreed over the matter of intellectual property rights. Consequently, Clinton threatened to cut off billions in Chinese exports to the United States if China refused to end its piracy of American movies, music, and software. Heading into the midterm election of 1994, American–Chinese relations remained fractious and turbulent, with little or no indication that either side had found a way to reach agreement on a matter of deep concern to both parties.

The United States and Russia, on the other hand, appeared to have established the basis for a stable partnership in the first years of the Clinton administration. A key to that arrangement was the growing rapport between Bill Clinton and Boris Yeltsin, the Russian president. Clinton initially supported his market-oriented, democratic reforms and provided Yeltsin with over $4 billion to help ease the wrenching transition from a command economy to one driven by the ethos of a free market. But that sum, in addition to whatever else Moscow received from the West, did little good in making for a smooth transition to a new and better world for most Russians.

During the Yeltsin years, the Russian people suffered from massive corruption, growing mob influence, and gangster-style warfare over economic turf. Notwithstanding those untoward developments, Clinton stood by Yeltsin, needing his support for the ratification of the START II treaty in the Russian Duma, which would make possible the dismantling of large numbers of nuclear weapons still in Russian hands. At the same time that Russia was engulfed by both economic and political turmoil, American oil companies were busily pursuing new economic opportunities in the vast resource-rich gas and oil states of the former Soviet Union, located in central Asia and now independent of Moscow's control and rule.

Although Clinton had no choice but to confront those foreign policy issues, he remained fixated on a domestic policy agenda in 1994, where for him the political stakes were the highest. Despite an upturn in the economy in early 1994, he had to worry about possible voter rejection in 1994 because too many Americans still saw little or no evidence of any real improvement in their daily lives. Not helping matters was Alan Greenspan, who worried that the decline of unemployment to a little more than 6 percent could spark the renewal of inflation. Consequently, he raised interest rates several times in early and midspring of 1994, even though inflation was nowhere in sight. By attacking a nonexistent enemy, Greenspan's action had the potential to dampen the fragile recovery then underway, but the Clinton administration dared not publicly question his policy to any great extent. It did not want to antagonize such a powerful individual, who was in a position to determine the future course of the American economy as well as Clinton's political fate.

In the meantime, the president had his hands full with internal administrative matters as well as with renewed difficulties on Capitol Hill. The chaos in the White House reflected the way Clinton did his business, and it eventually forced him to appoint Leon Panetta, the current budget director, as chief of staff, replacing his boyhood friend Thomas McLarty. But Clinton's more serious problems lay elsewhere, in Congress and in the court of public opinion. His health bill had been scuttled, his welfare bill was introduced too late in the session to bring it to legislative resolution, and his crime bill was in deep trouble in the House.

The welfare bill had serious problems, not the least of which was the strong opposition it engendered among many liberal Democrats, who feared that it might threaten the entitlement feature of the current legislation or impose time limits on benefits. Most likely, they agreed with Senator Moynihan's characterization of Clinton's proposal as "boob bait for the bubbas" (a remark he later regretted making). For New Democrats, however, Clinton had initiated the process of welfare reform by offering a five-year package to help in the transition from welfare to workfare. So if Congress granted Clinton the $9.3 billion he requested to implement his program, the funds would have been spent on training programs, child care, and job subsidies. On the other hand, the bill that he submitted to Congress in June 1994 would also have imposed a two-year lifetime limit for those receiving welfare benefits. Because of the deep division among Democrats in Congress, Clinton's bill never received a serious legislative review. Yet as a result of Clinton's stance, "welfare reform" had now been placed on the table for future congressional consideration and action.

Clinton's crime legislation responded to the continuing fear of street violence, which many voters equated with the deadly use of firearms. At a time when his support in the country was rapidly ebbing, he fought hard for passage of a bill that included the following provisions: a ban on the sale of nineteen different assault weapons, a "three strikes and you're out" feature for federal crimes, funding for new prison construction, and the placing of 100,000 new police officers on the streets. Although the GOP nearly denied him a legislative victory in the House, Clinton managed to get his measure through Congress, which gave him an opportunity to burnish his New Democratic credentials. Politically driven, Clinton's bill was directed at suburban America, which was the audience he wanted to reach while in his crime-fighting mode. A clever ploy, it also was part of a legislative strategy designed to co-opt a key Republican issue on which Democrats had been vulnerable for decades. Given the political priorities of this administration, it did not matter that Clinton's bill offered little relief to the inner cities, where most violent street crime occurred.

In the meantime, the 1994 midterm election was on the horizon, and Bill Clinton was at the heart of the debate now taking place in the country. As a result of his failure to deliver a middle-class tax cut, his stance on both guns and gays, and his inability to successfully sell his health reform package or to push welfare reform through Congress, his poll ratings were at 40 percent in the late summer of 1994. In addition, the controversy surrounding Whitewater and the Paula Jones lawsuit diminished the respect some citizens had for their recently elected chief executive.

Such was Clinton's standing that his presidency had become the target of a stream of bitingly sarcastic remarks delivered by Rush Limbaugh, the powerful voice of conservative radio. And in a more humorous but still deadly fashion, Jay Leno of *The Tonight Show* also captured something of that growing national disdain for Clinton, remarking: "At a town meeting in Rhode Island, President Clinton said that there were powerful forces threatening to bring down his administration. I think that they are called hormones." Surely these radio and television comments were symptomatic of deeper political, economic, and cultural trends at work inside American society, indicating that Clinton and his fellow Democrats were in trouble with the electorate.

Republicans had been doing well even before the November election, having triumphed at the polls in 1993 and early 1994. They won the major races in the off-year election of 1993, including a Senate seat in Texas, the contests for mayor in New York City and Los Angeles, as well as races for governor in New Jersey and Virginia. Possibly more ominous for the Democrats were the results of a special congressional election in Kentucky in May 1994, where they lost a seat that they had held for 129 years. There, the Republican victory resulted from a massive grassroots mobilization by the Christian Coalition, a staunchly conservative organization committed to a pro-life agenda and prayer in the public schools.

While the GOP was scoring victories at the polls, the congressional Republican leadership had managed to tie up the legislative process in such a way as to prevent the passage of key Democratic bills designed to reform lobbying practices and campaign finance laws. As Clinton's stock sank, Republicans prepared for a competitive race for control of Congress, knowing that their chances for victory had improved, especially since many more Americans now felt that the GOP could do better than the Democrats in managing the economy.

How ironic that Clinton's stewardship of the economy seemed to leave much to be desired. Since he had taken office, the deficit had been reduced from $290 billion to $228 billion, several million new jobs had been created, and unemployment had dropped by nearly a full point. Yet most Americans, in September 1994, did not believe that the deficit had been lowered. So Clinton got little credit on that score. And even though there had been an improvement in the economy, a majority of workers had not fully benefited from that development: they still worried about the continuing downsizing of corporate America, and their wages remained stagnant.

Secretary of Labor Robert Reich later sought to address those concerns when he referred to an "anxious middle class" whose interests needed protection in order to ensure the stability and the well-being of the American commonwealth. But his prescriptions would have required the expenditure of many billions to provide the safety net workers needed in an age of globalization. And that kind of money was simply not available, given the Clinton administration's budgetary priorities, which were dictated partially by the caps imposed by Congress and partially by its own earlier commitment to deficit reduction and new spending programs for the military.

Throughout his first two years in office, Clinton had eagerly courted business elites while working for the passage of NAFTA, deficit reduction, and the opening of new markets in a global context. Yet those business elites gave him little political support, feeling that his core domestic policies were still too liberal and too intrusive for their taste. Carrying this view to a much higher level of absurdity, Newt Gingrich, the House Republican Whip, denounced Clinton as the most left-wing president of the twentieth century. Countering that charge, Canadian journalist Graham Fraser noted that Clinton was a president who "supports free trade, capital punishment, throwing people off welfare after two years, health care that preserves the role of private insurance companies and requires everyone to pay premiums, and a massive increase in prison constructions and the number of police on the streets."

Although Gingrich's charge was rhetorically preposterous, his tactical shrewdness was clearly evident when he organized a gathering of Republican candidates running for House seats to meet on the Capitol steps in late September 1994 to sign what he called a Contract with America. Seeking to use this event as a way to nationalize the election with an anti-Clinton agenda, Gingrich included in his Contract a balanced budget amendment, welfare reform, a line-item veto for the president, added funding for the military, term limits, tighter crime control measures, and tax cuts that included a 50 percent reduction in the capital gains tax. By avoiding such divisive issues as abortion and prayer in the public schools, he sought to unify the party around an agenda that would be acceptable to moderates and conservatives alike.

Although most Americans never heard of the Contract with America, as it was spelled out that September day, Democrats naively thought that it might help their congressional campaigns in the belief that the GOP had given them an easy target to hit. Yet the dismay and disgust with Clinton, resulting from his support of gays in the military as well as gun control, and his effort to legislate a big government health reform, was so strong among voters that Stan Greenberg, Clinton's 1992 pollster, advised Democratic candidates to avoid any identification with him.

Clinton, while campaigning that fall, sought to mobilize support, especially from Perot voters, by stressing that he had reduced the number of government employees to levels not seen since the Kennedy presidency and that deficit reduction was now well under way. But results of the election demonstrated that his message did him and his party little good. The Republicans, having fully mobilized their base on the right, crushed the Democrats and seized control of Congress for the first time since 1952. Some observers viewed the magnitude of the Republican victory as having historic significance. Harvard political scientist Harvey Mansfield, for one, saw in the GOP takeover of Congress "the end of the New Deal" and "the completion of what Ronald Reagan began."

Although only 38.7 percent of eligible voters turned out to vote, the anti-Clinton tide ran everywhere and probably contributed to the defeat of such Democratic governors as Mario Cuomo of New York and Ann

Richards of Texas. It was especially strong in the South, where the GOP now established a strong base in a majority of congressional districts to complement its already ample presidential assets in the same region. Outside the South, the GOP also did remarkably well and even defeated House Speaker Thomas Foley. All in all, seventy-four Republican freshmen were elected to the House, which made for a fairly secure Republican majority in that chamber. At the same time, the Republicans won control of the Senate.

The Democrats were also hurt by the fact that the economic improvement during 1994 did not trickle down far enough to improve the stagnant wages of poorly educated single women and male high school graduates. Uninspired by Clinton or his record, they failed to turn out for Democratic candidates in numbers to stem the GOP tide. This was especially true for many black voters in swing districts around the country. At the same time, however, Republican voters were effectively mobilized by the Christian Coalition and the National Rifle Association, and they went to the polls in numbers throughout the country.

The politics of cultural resentment and antigovernment sentiment clearly played a significant role in augmenting that Republican vote. One Republican House freshman—Mark Souder of Indiana—later described the social groups that had come together to express to him their frustration and anger with the president's leadership and policies. Clinton had

> managed to unite doctors, insurers, gun owners, religious conservatives, motorcyclists, smokers, country-club Republicans, and blue-collar workers. [Going to meetings, I] would find guys rising with long-hair, tattoos, and a cigarette who were agreeing with me! People were upset by motorcycle helmet laws and smoking restrictions. These people were fed up with the intrusion of the federal government.

Republicans, given the results of the election, were eager to push ahead with their agenda—as spelled out in the Contract with America. Democrats, including a demoralized President Clinton, were in a state of shock, and they lacked a comparable agenda to cope with the legislative program and fresh energy now driving an elated Republican Party. Thus, on the eve of the GOP takeover of the incoming 104th Congress, many wondered whether Bill Clinton, like George Bush before him, was destined to serve only one term as president.

Chapter Three

Clinton's Comeback

Many newly elected House Republicans, having successfully nationalized the midterm election of 1994, came to Washington in January 1995 believing that voters had given them a mandate to roll back the power and reach of the national government. As modern-day antifederalists, they viewed federal power as a threat to the authority and freedom of the fifty states and local communities; thus, they were committed to passing legislation to advance the process of devolution. At the same time, they strongly endorsed a balanced budget and tax cuts. For them a balanced budget was key to reaching other objectives. As House Speaker Newt Gingrich explained it, balancing the budget "changes the whole game. . . .You cannot sustain the old welfare state inside a balanced budget."

Although Gingrich was the principal leader of House Republicans, he did not rule entirely by fiat: there were competing interests and outlooks that he had to confront and reconcile in order to prevent that majority from splintering into unruly factions. Hence, he was less ideologically driven than many of the new members of the House who were elected in 1994 from the South and Southwest, which had now become the new heartland of House Republicans. And unlike more moderate Republicans from the Northeast, they were largely committed to the outlook and values of entrepreneurial business, the conservative Christian Coalition, and the National Rifle Association, which all functioned as major grassroots organizers, as well as sources of campaign funds for those on the Republican right.

Pushed by these newly elected militants, the House GOP was rife with partisan passion and eager to do battle with the Clinton White

House and the legacy of the Great Society. And given its determination to change the face and function of the federal government, it was in no mood for compromise, believing that its agenda, as spelled out in the Contract with America, would form a legislative record that the voting public would willingly accept and support. Whether that was the case or merely wishful thinking on their part would soon be put to the test.

As House Republicans began work on efforts to dismantle the infrastructure of the welfare state, the White House remained in a state of shock, having lost its footing and confidence as a result of the midterm election. Although President Clinton once again endorsed a tax cut for the middle class and an increase in the minimum wage, he was fundamentally uncertain about what direction to move or what programs to push in order to reclaim the political ground lost as a result of the defeat in the midterm election. As the political center of gravity shifted to Congress, it now appeared that the president had become a passive participant in policy debates in Washington.

Confusion and demoralization were also evident among House Democrats, who, like Clinton, were stunned by losing a majority they had retained since 1954. With a president they neither liked nor trusted, and lacking an agenda of their own, House Democrats sought to find their way by opposing Republican legislation. Their strategy, put simply, was to highlight the social costs of the new GOP agenda to various claimants on the federal purse. By attacking the Republicans via "negative" politics, they hoped to restore cohesion and purpose to a caucus whose complexion and character had changed with the defeat of many southern moderates in 1994. Decidedly more liberal than before that election, House Democrats now differed with the president on a number of key matters, including tactics for countering the Republican revolution.

For the Republicans, a tax cut, which was especially designed to provide benefits for their affluent constituents in suburban America, was "the crown jewel" of the Contract. They also knew that such a cut, along with a requirement for a balanced budget by the year 2002, would surely deprive the federal government of the financial resources necessary to fund such entitlement programs as Medicare and Medicaid at their current levels. Given this dual objective, Republican John Kasich, chair of the House Budget Committee, had to find ways of cutting $600 billion from federal spending over the next five years. Yet if he were to succeed in carrying out his appointed task, many interest groups, including the working poor, would lose a vital resource base, but government itself would be diminished.

As House Republicans began to draft their budget, the Democrats, beginning to battle for position, pointed out that Republican programs included cuts in mandatory funding for school lunch programs, which affected not only poor children but middle-class children as well. And after also citing Republican efforts to reduce spending on Medicare, they were encouraged to discover that the public had gotten the message. Poll data now revealed growing support for their position, suggesting that Republicans might have misjudged how far they could go in attacking such programs. That shift also indicated that although a majority may have had little love for government in the abstract, they were determined not to lose benefits and supports that Washington provided. So if most Americans were ideologically conservative in this period, they remained operationally liberal, especially when their vital interests and personal security were at stake.

Meanwhile, Bill Clinton, who had already broken several campaign promises, was in deep political trouble. Although he still retained the advantage of incumbency and the power of the veto, his future prospects were uncertain. Many congressional Democrats distrusted him, and the House Republicans believed that he lacked the political standing and will necessary to challenge their attack on government. Moreover, those same Republicans were also convinced that the election of 1994 had given them a mandate to function as the governing party. Led by Speaker Gingrich, they operated in a highly partisan manner and saw no need to compromise with either the White House or Democrats on Capitol Hill.

Clinton's dilemma was simple enough: he found himself locked in controversy and conflict with forces from both directions. On one side were liberal Democrats, with whom he had a shaky relationship on both a personal and a political level. On the other were conservative Republicans, who had triumphed at the polls in 1994 with views to his right on deficit reduction, a balanced budget, lower taxes, welfare reform, crime legislation, and spending cuts for Medicare. Finding his way, then, through this political minefield would require a display of political dexterity and skill that Clinton had yet to demonstrate since coming to the White House.

Realizing that he was in an untenable political situation, Clinton once more called on Dick Morris, an old political consultant and adviser from his Arkansas days, to provide him with a strategy to strengthen his reelection prospects. An astute professional operator who had worked in the past with liberal Democrats and conservative Republicans alike, Morris, after examining Clinton's situation, believed that the president had to distance himself from both his congressional Democratic colleagues and the GOP. Morris also saw that Clinton's interest would be better served if he combined ideas and programs from both sides. In Morris's mind, that meant the creation of "a third position, not just between the old positions of the two parties, but above them as well." The tactical means of obtaining that third position would be determined by the extensive use of polling data.

As a part of the strategy, Morris helped draft a speech that Clinton delivered in Dallas in early April 1995, which spelled out a defense of his presidency. There, he also denounced the House Republican tax bill as a "fantasy" and its welfare reform bill as "weak on work, tough on kids." Describing himself as "the dynamic center," Clinton stated that he had not been elected president to "pile up a stack of vetoes" and that he was still hoping to get things done while searching for common ground with the GOP.

This speech marked the beginning of a serious effort by Clinton to work his way back to respectability at a time when his current and long-term prospects looked dim. Not only did he face a strong possibility of a challenge in the coming primaries, but his current standing was so low that several of the major television networks refused to carry his live press conference on the evening of April 18, 1995. During that press conference (at a time when Newt Gingrich appeared to be running the government from the Speaker's chair in the House chamber), Clinton was reduced to saying that because the Constitution had given him authority and standing, "the President is relevant here."

The next day, on April 19, 1995, a bomb planted by a domestic terrorist exploded severely damaging a federal building in Oklahoma City and killing 168 people. Suddenly, the president had an opportunity to revise his public image. Later that day, Clinton declared: "We will find the people who did this. When we do, justice will be swift, certain, and severe." On April 21, two days after the bombing, Timothy McVeigh, a former serviceman with links to right-wing paramilitary groups, was placed in custody, charged with having committed that heinous crime.

Clinton's moving speech at the memorial service in Oklahoma City for the bombing victims provided an opportunity for the country to see him functioning as a leader. The bombing also gave Clinton an opportunity to target the purveyors of hate and violence. In Minneapolis he denounced "those loud and angry voices in America today whose sole goal seems to be to try to keep some people as paranoid as possible and the rest of us torn up and upset with each other. They spread hate. They leave the impression by their very words that violence is acceptable." Notwithstanding the pervasive climate of opinion in the country about the insidious character of government (fueled by conservative talk-radio hosts), Clinton's appeal to moderates and his rejection of extremist rhetoric went over well. An NBC News/Wall Street Journal poll, released the day after his Minneapolis speech, revealed that 84 percent of respondents approved his handling of the Oklahoma City tragedy. As a White House aide remarked, "In Oklahoma, we just hit."

In the meantime, Newt Gingrich and his fellow Republicans, unfazed and unmoved by Clinton's rhetoric, remained determined to push ahead with their agenda, which included tax cuts, a reduction in the size of government, and a balanced budget. And driving them forward was their conviction that it was possible to accomplish all this and still retain voter confidence.

Clinton, feeling heat from Gingrich and the voters over a balanced budget, and needing to appear reasonable while staking out his own position on an important legislative matter, had earlier submitted a budget that retained a $200 billion deficit without suggesting when the budget would be brought into balance. After receiving the advice of Dick Morris and Vice President Al Gore, however, he submitted, on June 13, 1995, a fresh plan for a balanced budget in ten years, which required not only a reduction in spending of over $1 trillion but also included both a middle-class tax cut and a proposed savings of $125 billion from Medicare.

Once Clinton announced his new budget, congressional Democrats instantly felt betrayed, for they had strongly opposed such a move, as did several of Clinton's key advisers, fearing that it would undercut their campaign to save current spending levels for Medicare, which had proven popular with the voters. The question arose: Why did Clinton act in a way that alienated members of his own party in Congress? According to Dick Morris, Clinton needed a proposal not only to separate himself from his fellow Democrats but, more important, to deprive the GOP of the issue. In short, by accepting the goal of a balanced budget (a Republican objective), he would be in a stronger position to defend important Democratic programs from a harsh and unbalanced Republican onslaught directed against the idea of government. For Clinton, the argument with the Republicans would now concern how to achieve the goal, not whether it ought to be done. In that context, the politics of triangulation had come of age, thanks to Dick Morris, its leading exponent in the Clinton White House.

As the battle of the budget between the White House and Congress actively commenced in the late summer of 1995, Clinton began to shore up his position in other areas. Critical in this regard was his desire to establish centrist positions on "values" issues such as crime, television violence, prayer in the public schools, cigarette sales to minors, and affirmative action. Encouraged by Morris and his polling data, he gave a series of "common ground" speeches spelling out where he stood on such matters. In one such speech, for example, Clinton effectively aborted a Republican effort to push for a constitutional amendment permitting prayer in the public schools by calling for a study of religion in the public schools. And he carefully raised the matter of excessive television violence without endorsing the need for hard regulation, a proposition his otherwise loyal financial backers in Hollywood would surely have rejected.

Most important, Clinton shrewdly took off the table what might have been for him a potentially dangerous debate over affirmative action. That is, if he failed to support the continuation of affirmative action programs, which was a high-priority item for many black Americans, it might have led Jesse Jackson to enter the Democratic primaries to oppose him for the party's nomination. Very much aware of that possibility, and also aware that Republicans might use it as a wedge issue in 1996, Clinton spoke at the National Archives on July 19, 1995, and stated the case for keeping affirmative action.

If there had been problems in the past with the program, he said, the basic objective was to mend it, not end it. At the same time, he repeated his opposition to quotas and racial preferences. Having made his case in a manner that appealed to different groups at the same time, Clinton was reassured by Morris's polling data, which revealed that a solid majority of both blacks and whites felt that he had not favored one race over another.

As Clinton sought to make political headway with values issues, he had not yet recovered from the debacle of 1994. A New York Times/CBS News poll in August 1995 found that retired General Colin Powell, a possible Republican presidential challenger, was running ten points ahead of Clinton and that Republican Senator Bob Dole was leading him by six points. At the same time, only 45 percent of those polled approved of the way he was doing his job, while a mere 41 percent endorsed his handling of the economy. Ominously for Clinton, a mere 14 percent felt that the economy was improving, as against 27 percent who thought it was getting worse.

Clinton had not been helped by the restrictive monetary policy pursued by Alan Greenspan, the chairman of the Federal Reserve Board. Much to the consternation of the White House, Greenspan had raised interest rates from early 1994 to early 1995 as unemployment began to drop, because he feared it would soon spark an inflationary renewal. But by mid-1995, with no inflation in sight, he proceeded to lower those interest rates, which helped to fuel the historic economic and stock market boom to come. In practice, then, Greenspan had taken a step that ran counter to current economic theory and past economic behavior, which automatically assumed a natural and law-like relationship between unemployment rates below the 6.4 percent range and heightening inflation. But since unemployment continued to decline and inflation remained virtually nonexistent, something different was ostensibly at work inside the American economy. Greenspan, to his credit, responded to that situation by ignoring past economic models and explanations that clearly did not fit the new empirical reality.

Deficit reduction, along with lower interest rates, had also encouraged further investment and growth. Thus, those officials, led by Treasury Secretary Robert Rubin (Lloyd Bentsen's successor) and Alan Greenspan who had argued for the policy in late 1992 and 1993 now appeared vindicated in their judgment. But whether this was enough to satisfy voters who had yet to benefit from either deficit reduction or the surge of growth was another matter. Despite the fact that several million new jobs had been created since 1993, that corporate profits had jumped considerably over their 1993 levels, and that both unemployment and the deficit were on their way down, many Americans still worried about their economic futures. They had read the stories about how blue-ribbon corporations, such as IBM, General Motors, and General Electric, were continuing to slash their workforces and eliminating tens of thousands of middle-management jobs throughout corporate America.

As corporate downsizing accelerated for those in middle-management positions, job losses for blue-collar workers in the manufacturing sector continued unabated. Undergoing a massive structural transformation since the 1980s, manufacturing now utilized only 18 percent of the workforce, as key industries such as steel and autos, seeking to cope with globalization, resorted to automating the work process in order to reduce their labor costs. In turn, this meant that many fewer full-time jobs at decent salaries were now available for blue-collar workers, unlike the situation in industrial America two decades earlier. And even if those technologically displaced workers found other jobs, usually their salaries were now considerably lower and that their health benefits and pensions had shrunk or had been lost altogether.

During this same period, service sector jobs in the retail market had expanded greatly, but they were often jobs that did not pay very much beyond the minimum wage. Confirming those developments were the findings of the Dunlop Commission on the Future of Worker/ Management Relations, which had been created jointly by Secretary of Labor Robert Reich and Secretary of Commerce Ron Brown. It reported in mid-1994 that the number of low-wage workers has "grown greatly, with the result that a sizable proportion of U.S. workers are paid markedly less than comparable workers in other advanced countries." And it went on to acknowledge that the "real" hourly compensation of American workers had stagnated over the past two decades and had actually fallen for male workers, a development "unprecedented in the past 75 years in this country." Surely, the weakness of organized labor as a significant defender of worker rights had something to do with the sad economic state of many American workers, which the Dunlop Commission had spelled out.

The decline of the American labor movement did not begin in the Clinton years. That development could be traced back several decades, reaching a culmination of sorts in the Reagan years, when a Republican administration decertified a union that had launched an illegal strike against the government in 1981. In addition, the Reagan administration had loaded the National Labor Relations Board (NLRB) with appointees hostile to the union movement. But even more far-reaching was the impact of globalization on the American labor movement; it came at a time when the AFL-CIO was already suffering from a rapidly falling membership in relation to the rest of the workforce. But because a tired labor leadership, headed by Lane Kirkland, lacked the energy or direction to undertake a fresh grass-roots mobilization to help revitalize the labor movement, it had few internal resources to cope with those vast changes in the structure of the American and international economy.

Despite its many troubles, labor's long-term institutional relationship with the Democratic Party remained fairly constant. Over the decades, it had provided organizational help and money to help elect Democrats to public office in Washington, thereby becoming a vital cog in the party's election machinery. In a practical sense, most northern Democrats in Congress understood that their political interests and labor's agenda generally converged, but not always. In Clinton's case, however, there was a period of strong friction between labor and the White House as a result of his embracing NAFTA and his failure to work hard for the passage of the Striker Replacement Act of 1994. But Clinton's appointment of pro-labor lawyer William Gould to head the NLRB, his later support for an increase in the minimum wage, and his preventing the GOP from greatly weakening, if not destroying, the Occupational Health and Safety Administration eased matters and brought him back into the good graces of labor.

By mid-1995, Clinton and labor began to work toward a common goal of defeating Republicans in 1996. And aiding in that process was John Sweeney's election in October 1995 as head of the AFL-CIO. Deploring labor's fall from "political powerhouse to political patsy," he announced the reactivation of labor's role in national politics. Consequently, the membership of the AFL-CIO was assessed $25 million to underwrite an advertising campaign on behalf of, and to provide financial assistance for, candidates opposed to Gingrich's Contract.

As the Clinton administration and organized labor reconciled their differences, the Republican Congress had not yet worked out the full details of the federal budget for the new fiscal year, which was scheduled to begin October 1, 1995. In the interim, Congress passed a continuing resolution designed to keep the government operating at its current fiscal level for departments and agencies that had not yet been funded for the new fiscal year. But in the event Congress failed to renew that resolution, or in case it passed a fresh one that the president then proceeded to veto, the government would face a partial shutdown of services.

The politics of the budget, meanwhile, dominated policy matters at the White House. On October 19, Clinton announced that he now was committed to the goal of a balanced budget in seven years, as determined by the Office of Management and Budget (OMB). In short, he had accepted Gingrich's target goal, but not his instrument of the Congressional Budget Office (CBO) to score his plan. At the same time, however, Clinton emphasized the need to protect certain key programs such as Medicare from a Republican attack.

Clinton's defense of Medicare notwithstanding, the Republican Congress included in its new continuing resolution a provision eliminating a scheduled drop in Medicare premiums. In another bill authorizing the raising of the ceiling on the federal debt limit, it also included a rider weakening the reach of federal regulatory power and a provision for a balanced budget by 2002 as scored by the CBO. Much to Gingrich's surprise, Clinton refused to blink, vetoing both bills as bad public policy. In the absence of a new resolution, a partial shutdown of government services commenced on November 14, 1995.

Why did such a train wreck occur? Put simply, Gingrich and his fellow Republicans had grossly miscalculated the politics of the shutdown. As poll data revealed, the American people had become more and more disenchanted with much of the Republican agenda. And nowhere was this more evident than with respect to the issue of protecting Medicare. Clinton, reading the polls, knew he held a strong hand on this issue, and so he acted accordingly.

Once the government closed its doors, both sides began to negotiate the basis for another continuing resolution. Especially important was Gingrich's removal of the Medicare proposal from the proposed resolution: he wanted the matter of a balanced budget to be the focal point of the discussion. At the time, the pressure was on Clinton to act, as his approval ratings in the polls were dropping. Also, some House Democrats, fearing that they would be held accountable for opposing a balanced budget agreement, wanted him to sign that resolution. But because he was worried about a possible override of another veto, which would make him appear weak, Clinton accepted the principle of a balanced budget in seven years as determined by the CBO, and agreed to sign a new resolution. Thus, the government resumed operations after having been closed for six days. Nevertheless, unless Congress and the

White House could agree on a budget deal, or unless there was a joint agreement to support another continuing resolution, this new resolution was scheduled to expire on December 15, 1995.

Clinton's acceptance of a seven-year balanced budget as determined by the CBO, not the OMB, made it appear that Gingrich had won the strategic battle, even though Clinton contended that his key programs such as Medicare and education still remained protected under the agreement. In reality Clinton had come a long way in yielding high ground to the Republicans, and they recognized it. Speaking for most Republicans, Congressman John Kasich claimed, "we could see that they had accepted our bookends — seven years and CBO." And that, after all, was the heart of the matter at this stage of the budget battle.

While a short-term agreement had been reached to reopen the government, Gingrich, concurrently, was taking a terrible beating in the polls. Now viewed by many Americans as an extremist, he had become the most unpopular politician in the country. Also doing him damage was the character and content of the new Republican budget, which had cleared Congress after both houses had reconciled their differences. In many ways that legislation, which the president had already promised to veto, constituted the high-water mark of the Republican revolution. It called for a balanced budget by the year 2002, a Medicare cut of $270 billion over a seven-year period, and a tax cut of $245 billion for mostly upper-income Americans. In addition, many current federal programs such as welfare and Medicaid were scheduled to be transferred back to the states through a system of block grants, while funding for other social programs, largely benefiting the working poor, would be either substantially reduced or eliminated altogether. As this budget went through the legislative process, it represented a concerted Republican effort, centered in the House, to roll back, if not destroy, the federal welfare state with fiscal policy. Praising the handiwork of Congress, Gingrich aptly remarked, "This is the largest domestic decision we made since 1933. . . . This is a fundamental change in the direction of government." But President Clinton, unwilling to countenance a radical shift of that magnitude in the function of government, vetoed the Republican budget on December 6, 1995.

Because it lacked either a fixed budget or another continuing resolution extending beyond December 15, the government once more was forced to partially close its doors for a second time, which denied the public access to the national parks or government museums in Washington. Those doors remained shut for the next twenty-one days. During that period, both sides sought to reach an agreement, but their respective positions were fundamentally at odds with one another. Gingrich and his House caucus demanded that Clinton submit a budget in accord with a seven-year balance scored by the CBO. At the same time, Clinton was under intense pressure from Democrats on Capitol Hill not to sell out Medicare and other programs to which they were committed, nor to accept the deep Republican tax cut. But when Clinton finally submitted a balanced budget by 2002 as scored by the CBO, it proved unsatisfactory to House Republicans, who wanted deeper cuts in Medicare and taxes than he was willing to countenance. Though both sides were not that far apart in their respective Medicare figures, the differences between them on other matters such as taxes proved too difficult to bridge. Hence, negotiations were suspended in early January 1996.

Meanwhile, the GOP was falling behind in the polls, while Clinton's standing with the public was on the rise. Aware of that development, the Republican leadership in the House and Senate decided to open the government in early January 1996 after the CBO declared that the budget Clinton had submitted to them would indeed be balanced in seven years. At that point, Congress began to fund those departments and agencies still lacking their appropriations for the current fiscal year. Thus, despite the lack of a final budget agreement for fiscal 1996, there would be no further shutdown of the government. Having closed it twice, Gingrich and House Republicans had paid a high price for their convictions. Victims of ideological absolutism, they had profoundly miscalculated the public's desire to roll back government at the expense of the entitlement programs and government services that mattered to most Americans. Like Clinton in 1993–94, they had overreached their mandate in 1995. Many voters viewed them as extremists who wanted to cut Medicare and other programs simply to provide tax cuts for the rich. Yet Clinton himself had moved a long way from where he was in 1993 to a point where he now agreed with the need to strike a balanced budget in seven years, tied to significant reductions in government spending for social programs.

His concession notwithstanding, Clinton had rebounded from near political death in early 1995 to a strong contending position for reelection by early 1996, thanks to a government shutdown and his agile handling of the negotiations during the budget crisis. Also, several actions he had taken in the area of foreign policy during 1995 helped him to recover his political balance and added to his stature as a president capable of making hard decisions and of providing much-needed leadership. For example, in the face of strong opposition from Congress, he approved a $20 billion loan to Mexico from emergency funds at his disposal, which helped stabilize the peso. He also continued to support the Oslo Accord between Israel and the Palestine Liberation Organization, which had opened the door for a possible long-term reconciliation and settlement between the two sides. In addition, he embraced the policy of strategic engagement with China, hoping in this way to settle basic disagreements with Beijing over trade and copyright protection for American intellectual and cultural commodities, while seeking to avoid a diplomatic breakdown over Taiwan.

But developments in Bosnia soon transcended those other foreign policy issues in importance. Given his legislative priorities at the time, he focused primarily on domestic economic matters, even as the crisis in Bosnia drifted ever more dangerously. Confused and uncertain as to what steps he should take, he refused to endorse the Vance-Owens plan creating ten separate cantons in Bosnia (divided among Bosnian Serb, Croat, and Muslim entities) on the grounds that it violated the right of self-determination. And although Clinton proposed something along the lines of "lift and strike," he later backed off from the policy after it was vetoed by the British and French. Instead, he now favored not lifting the arms embargo on the Bosnian Muslims, while opposing American air strikes on Serb positions in Bosnia.

Clinton's policy reflected the views of a majority of Americans, who believed that any future military mission involving ground troops had to be in the vital interest of the United States. Most Americans did not deem the crisis in Bosnia to be of that magnitude. Clinton, who constantly read the polls, knew it very well. Consequently, he was unwilling and unable to devise a policy that included a strong American military commitment to the region, leaving Britain and France to deal with the nightmare of ethnic cleansing in Bosnia without the help and support from NATO's most powerful member.

Yet the situation in Bosnia was not static. By the summer of 1995, Clinton suddenly realized that the deteriorating situation in the Balkans required his full attention, for he now saw that his political prospects at home and the credibility of American foreign policy were endangered by the continuation of that conflict. Making it imperative for him to move was the convergence of several developments that necessitated a fresh approach. They included a threat from the British and French to pull their troops out of Bosnia, which would have required the American army to assist them; the passage of a possible veto-proof resolution in Congress calling for the lifting of the arms embargo on Bosnian Muslims; the slaughter of thousands of Bosnian Muslim males by Bosnian Serbian gunmen at Srebrenica in early July; and finally, a warning from Dick Morris and others to Clinton that he had to take Bosnia off the table quickly, or it could hurt his reelection prospects in 1996.

Although each of these factors was compelling, the shelling of Sarajevo by Bosnian Serbs on August 28, 1995, brought everything to a head, leading Clinton to push immediately for NATO air strikes on Serb positions. Next came his diplomatic effort, culminating in the Dayton Accord, which Deputy Secretary of State Richard Holbrooke had successfully brokered in Ohio. Holbrooke's arduous negotiation ended the conflict and provided the basis for the creation of a quasi-partitioned Bosnia. And to ensure compliance with the agreement, to which Slobodan Milosevic, the president of Serbia, and others were signatories, Clinton sent 20,000 American troops to Bosnia to act as peacekeepers, while promising that they would be withdrawn in a year's time. Because they were not going into combat, Dick Morris's polls indicated that the American people approved of their mission.

From Clinton's perspective, the timely ending of the Bosnian crisis was just what he needed to restore confidence in his leadership in both global and domestic contexts. Clinton's intervention laid to rest a charge made by Jacques Chirac of France that a "vacuum" existed at the top of NATO's command structure because of Clinton's refusal to act. And since Bosnia seemed settled, it would not prove troublesome in the 1996 presidential campaign. But at the same time, Kosovo, a province of Serbia, faced growing internal tension and conflict due to Belgrade's heavy-handed rule favoring the minority Serbs over the majority of Albanian Kosovars living there.

As Clinton headed into an election year, Kosovo was a mere blip on his radar screen. His primary business was to lay the groundwork for the reelection campaign to come. And helping him in that regard was the refusal of retired General Colin Powell to seek the Republican presidential nomination. Powell would have been a formidable opponent because of his popularity across racial and class lines. In that same vein, Clinton was also aided by the absence of a challenger in the Democratic primaries. Unlike early 1995, when he was in a very weakened position and fearful of such an attack from within his own party, Clinton had recovered enough political ground by early 1996 to have allayed that threat. He was now in a commanding position to win reelection, having escaped a fatal political derailment with the help of Newt Gingrich and Dick Morris.

Morris had provided the impetus for the repositioning of Clinton along more centrist lines than many of Clinton's other key White House advisers thought desirable. Against the more liberal policy proposals of George Stephanopoulos and Harold Ickes, Morris saw the political utility and necessity of co-opting Republican positions. It was his belief that by denying the GOP most of its key issues, such as support for a balanced budget, tougher crime legislation, and welfare reform, Clinton could "fast-forward the Gingrich agenda" to his political advantage. By doing so, he contended, the GOP would be left with little it could use as the basis of a successful multifaceted attack directed at the president in 1996.

Coupled with this shrewd tactical advice, which Clinton generally followed once it had been thoroughly poll-tested, was Morris's other stratagem: the development of a massive television advertising campaign, starting in the summer of 1995, to highlight Clinton's role in defending programs like Medicare, Social Security, and education and protecting the environment from attack by Republican "extremists." Morris eventually spent $85 million on those ads, which Clinton himself helped to design and draft. And they produced results, contributing to a steady improvement over time in Clinton's standing in the polls. Indeed, with the use of this tactic, Morris could rightly remark that he and his cohorts had created "the first fully advertised president in U.S. history."

Much to the amazement of Clinton campaign operatives, the GOP failed to respond to this early barrage, which Gingrich later admitted was "our biggest mistake." Overreaching may have been an even bigger mistake. Ignoring or disdaining public opinion polls, which captured the ambivalence Americans felt about government, Republicans in the House played their cards badly in the belief that that the public would eventually come to support their agenda and give them credit for doing the right thing. And they also misjudged Bill Clinton, thinking that he would give way and accept their demands in the face of a threatened government shutdown. Thanks to a double miscalculation, the Republican revolution had been stopped in its tracks by January 1996; angry voters now held Gingrich and his fellow Republicans responsible for seeking to cut Medicare funding and for creating the impasse that had led to two government shutdowns.

At the same time, though, Clinton understood that voters in 1996 wanted not just smaller government but the continuation of those vital services they associated with a welfare state for the middle class. Thus initiating a series of "bite-size" programs, Clinton sought to protect key government services while he addressed the matter of social values in a series of speeches designed to appeal to the important suburban swing voters. Thus, for example, in his 1996 State of the Union address, he proclaimed that "the era of big government is over." To underscore that point, he reassured his audience that government was now smaller and more efficient and that it functioned with many fewer workers than before. But he also reaffirmed that government must protect Social Security, Medicare, education, and the environment. At the heart of his speech, however, was Clinton's defense of family values, which included the responsibility of parents for their children and the need to control youth gangs, foster community policing, and reduce teen pregnancy and teen smoking. His emphasis on family values scored well in polls.

The economy was beginning to produce major benefits for many Americans in 1996. The stock market boomed, corporate profits soared, unemployment dropped, inflation appeared nonexistent, and interest rates stayed steady. Yet serious problems remained. Most upsetting for some was the continuation of corporate downsizing that, in the words of Secretary of Labor Robert Reich, had produced an "anxious class." Reich attacked "corporate welfare" and called for "corporate responsibility." But the administration, led by Secretary of the Treasury Robert Rubin, dismissed any attempt by Reich to impose new rules and regulations on corporate America via congressional legislation. At the same time, poll data revealed that although Americans worried about their jobs, they were not "necessarily in a corporate bashing mood," remaining more concerned with moral and social problems. Understandably, then, Clinton rejected a "class warfare strategy" in the spring of 1996 and opted for a more consensual approach, seeking cooperation between labor and business as the best way of coping with the problem of corporate downsizing.

The issues of wage stagnation and growing wealth and income inequality generally received less attention than corporate downsizing. By early 1996, despite the general improvement in the economy, there had been no appreciable improvement in real wages since the early 1970s, which was a fact of life for most working people caught up in the vicissitudes of the labor market. The steady increase in consumer debt for those situated from the middle to the bottom of the income scale added to the already heavy economic burden they had to carry. At the same time, the shift in wealth in an upward direction was even more telling. By 1996 the top 1 percent of household family units controlled nearly 40 percent of the nation's wealth, while the bottom 40 percent was left with two-tenths of 1 percent. It was a staggering difference that had been accelerating since the 1980s, and came at a time when 20 percent of American children continued to live in or near povertylike conditions.

Clinton had tried initially to ameliorate the conditions of the working poor by utilizing the earned income tax credit to provide them with a useful tax benefit, which by 1999 amounted to nearly $30 billion a year in subsidies. And he also had supported a shift in the marginal tax rates, which made them somewhat more progressive in character than they had been since the Reagan years. In addition, he called for a modest increase in the minimum wage, thereby endorsing John Sweeney's contention that "America needs a raise." When discussing the economy, Clinton informed the country that things were getting better for more people. He rarely focused on the darker side of the 1990s boom. Dick Morris's polling revealed that the country wanted to hear only optimistic and positive reports. Otherwise, warned Morris, there was a drop of 20 points in the polls whenever Clinton dealt with the economy's bleaker aspects as well as providing the encouraging uplift and spin that went along with the good news.

In the meantime, Clinton himself was experiencing good news. His job approval rating, according to New York Times/CBS News surveys, had steadily climbed above 50 percent after January 1996, which clearly strengthened his hand as he and his fellow Democrats prepared to face the Republican challenge in 1996. The Republicans, on the other hand, were smarting over the fact that Clinton had stolen their thunder on issue after issue, including a balanced budget and crime. One Republican expert on criminal justice, for example, referred to a bill restricting death row appeals that Clinton had signed, and observed, "We say habeas corpus; they say sure. We say prisons; they say sure. We say more firearms prosecutions; they say sure." Thus, with Clinton's policy of co-optation largely succeeding, the GOP was in a quandary as to how to attack this skillful and slick New Democratic president. Haley Barbour, chair of the Republican National Committee, tried to gain traction by pointing to the economy, hoping that it would serve as Clinton's Achilles' heel. "Clinton's high-tax, big-government policies," he remarked, "have sucked life out of the economy, eaten up American workers' pay and given money to the government instead. Clinton's policies have created the middle-class squeeze."

Actually, it was Clinton's squeeze on the Republicans that left them short of political breath. Various declared candidates for the GOP presidential nomination, including Senator Bob Dole, Patrick Buchanan, Steve Forbes, and Lamar Alexander, sought to fashion a message that might challenge Clinton. In the end, Dole, helped by the Republican establishment, eventually emerged as the GOP nominee. A mainstream, fiscally conservative Republican, he said that he was in the race because it was his turn to head the ticket. And if voters wanted him to be Reagan, he would be Reagan. Such was Dole's claim on the nomination as he prepared to leave the Senate in June 1996 to organize his campaign against Clinton.

Acting earlier in his capacity as the Senate's Majority Leader, Dole had to deal with Speaker Gingrich, whose tactics and more conservative House social agenda made Dole uncomfortable. Nevertheless, he generally went along with the House Republican leadership in order to demonstrate that he was an effective Senate leader and manager, while seeking to head off the challenge for the nomination from the more conservative Senator Phil Gramm. But unlike 1995, when he faced hard-line conservatives from the House who dominated the process and agenda, Dole found that House Republicans in 1996 were shifting their ground out of fear of voter retribution for the two government shutdowns and the cutbacks in various popular government programs. Seeking to regain a centrist appearance, they were now prepared to pass more moderate legislation that probably would not have stood a chance of acceptance a year earlier. But whether this helped Dole was another matter. By mid-1996, congressional Republicans were thinking more of enhancing their own reelection prospects with a more accommodating agenda, while taking steps to distance themselves from Dole's rapidly faltering presidential campaign.

Needing to appear reasonable and businesslike before the run-up to the election, this GOP tactical shift in Congress made possible the passage of such bipartisan centrist legislation as the Kennedy–Kassebaum portable health insurance bill, which Clinton had strongly endorsed earlier in the year. Put simply, it guaranteed that those individuals changing jobs would not lose the medical insurance they held in their prior job, but it put no ceiling on how much insurance companies could charge for their coverage. Nor did it provide the slightest protection for the more than forty million Americans who lacked medical insurance of any type.

At the same time that Congress took action on the Kennedy–Kassebaum bill, it also renewed the Safe Drinking Water Act and rewrote federal pesticide laws. More significant was the move to raise the minimum wage. Responding to a large majority in the country that wanted this legislation passed, Congress voted to increase the minimum wage from $4.25 an hour to $5.15. Coupled with that increase, however, was the inclusion of tax cuts for business, which made it easier to obtain the necessary votes for passage in Congress. Although the bill provided for only a modest raise, it was enough, perhaps, to encourage more people to look for work in the burgeoning service economy, which had become the major source of employment for those entering the labor market for the first time.

Americans generally approved of the increase in the minimum wage, hoping it would encourage people to seek employment and to profit from their work. In their view, work had a positive purpose, in that it affirmed "the American dream in material success through individual effort." This is why, on the other hand, many people generally condemned the welfare system as a bankrupt enterprise: in their opinion, it provided unearned and undeserved benefits for those who, they believed, preferred to stay on the welfare rolls rather than find a job.

Yet as historian Michael Katz points out, federal poverty programs had provided a helping hand for many impoverished Americans, raising some of them over the poverty line as well as lowering the infant mortality rate. But Aid to Families with Dependent Children (AFDC), a key welfare program that reached fourteen million recipients with a $23 billion price tag in 1995, had fallen into disrepute because of rampant in-

increases in crime, illegitimacy, and the rates of drug use, especially in the country's urban centers. The perception that money was being wasted on people who did not deserve handouts had become so widespread and deeply held that it gave Clinton an opportunity to score major political points with his pledge "to end welfare as we know it." But his proposal to legislate a different system based on public assistance to help people move from welfare to work, while putting time limits on benefits, had fallen prey to intense internal Democratic division and conflict in the 103rd Congress. Ironically, the GOP had introduced its own bill in that same Democratic Congress, which was not only similar to Clinton's but one that kept the entitlement feature of the federal program as well. As journalist Elizabeth Drew noted, here was an "unseized opportunity" for negotiations, which might have prevented the later demise of a federal program that provided the guarantee of limited financial protection and support for America's poorest children caught in the web of poverty.

By September 1995 it appeared that a major structural change in America's welfare program was on the way once the Republican-controlled Senate passed a welfare bill that won the support of a majority of Democrats, who came on board after Clinton endorsed the measure in principle. That particular bill imposed strict time limits on welfare and ended the entitlement aspect of the federal program, which dated back to New Deal days. In addition, it also proposed that more money be given to the states for child support. Suffice it to say that Clinton's quasi-endorsement of the Senate bill was a clear signal of his willingness to sign something so long as it did not appear punitive in substance and detail as did the House-drafted bill.

Although Clinton later vetoed two Republican-sponsored welfare bills on the grounds that they were simply too harsh, he faced a dilemma by the early summer of 1996. Republicans, determined to put him on the spot before the November election, had shrewdly excised from their latest bill all restrictions on Medicaid coverage for those low-income Americans qualified to receive it. Adamantly opposed to Republican efforts to weaken that program, Clinton now confronted a bill that was much harder for him to veto. Despite the strong opposition to this legislation from members of his own administration and from many Democrats in Congress, Clinton wanted to avoid any political damage that might ensue in the event he failed to honor his 1992 campaign promise "to end welfare as we know it."

Encouraged by Vice President Al Gore and Dick Morris not to veto the Personal Responsibility and Work Opportunity Reconciliation Act, Clinton, while recognizing the bill's "serious flaws," announced on July 31, 1996 that he would sign the legislation that Congress was sending to him. But he also said that he would work to correct those same flaws in the next Congress.

This new law constituted a sea change in American social policy. According to the *New York Times*, it

> ended the 60-year-old Federal guarantee of cash assistance for the nation's poorest children [AFDC], set a five-year limit on payments to any family, required most adult recipients to work within two years, and gave states vast new power to run their own welfare and work programs with sums of Federal money.

With its actions Congress had thus created fifty different welfare systems by passing the responsibility and administration of welfare on to the states via block grants. And in doing so, it expected to save $55 billion over the next six years, which, reported the *New York Times*, was derived from a "six-year, $24 billion cut in food stamp help to 25 million poor Americans and the barring of future legal immigrants from most welfare assistance." Clearly, then, the politics of devolution and the economics of cost-cutting had triumphed in the manner that Newt Gingrich and his associates had envisioned when they drafted the Contract with America.

Clinton had succeeded in getting the welfare monkey off his back, while paying homage to his New Democratic roots and "third-way" ideology. There were other problems that threatened his reelection campaign, including an ongoing congressional investigation of Whitewater, which seemed to suggest wrongdoing by the Clintons. Although nothing substantive was produced to damage either Bill Clinton or the first lady, Morris sought to smother all such allegations in the early summer of 1996 with a heavy barrage of campaign advertising that stressed Clinton's commitment to a "values" agenda. As a result of those ads, the president's polling numbers went up, and charges about Whitewater and various other matters affecting the operation of the White House virtually disappeared from view.

Clinton was also helped by a steady improvement in the economy, for which he finally received credit from many voters. Ten million new jobs had been created since 1993, unemployment had dropped well below 6 percent, the stock market soared, and corporate profits climbed at a rapid rate. At the same time, deficit reduction began to show real results, and interest rates remained stable because there was no inflation threat in sight. Thus, on the eve of the Republican Convention, Clinton was reassured about his election prospects, as everything that mattered in the domestic and international contexts had fallen into place for him.

That GOP Convention confirmed Bob Dole's nomination as the party's challenger for the presidency. In turn, Dole selected former Congressman Jack Kemp as his running mate. A staunch supporter of tax cuts, he also spoke for a more inclusive party, one that actively reached out to blacks and other minorities by supporting business initiatives for them from the private sector. The party platform also endorsed Dole's push for a 15 percent tax reduction as a way of unifying the party behind a common agenda. In addition, it also incorporated hard-line conservative positions on the most culturally divisive issues of the day, including abortion. A victory for the party's "theologians," it also was a stinging defeat for those moderates who wanted the GOP to adopt a more open pro-choice position on abortion in order to appeal to a majority of Americans who generally shared their position on that specific issue.

As a result of the GOP Convention, Dole managed to narrow the huge lead that Clinton had built up in the polls since the beginning of the year, but it did not last very long. Clinton had virtually restored his commanding lead over Dole by the time of the Democratic Convention in late August. On the other hand, it was not an entirely happy convention that came to Chicago to ratify the Clinton–Gore ticket. Clinton's signing of the welfare bill troubled many delegates, but they were prepared to live with it, given the likely prospect of their party's nominees winning a second term.

Clinton's acceptance speech and the party platform clearly reflected the changes that had taken place inside the Democratic Party since 1992. More in keeping with Clinton's New Democratic orientation, they both focused on the merits of deficit reduction, welfare reform, family values, and a smaller and more efficient government, as well as the need to protect Medicare, Social Security, education, and the environment from Republican "extremists." Virtually all of it was the product of a poll-driven agenda designed for the second term that Dick Morris had prepared for Clinton's election campaign.

The party platform also captured something of the split personality that had emerged inside the Democratic Party as a result of Clinton's stewardship. It declared that "what today's Democratic Party offers is the end of the era of big government, a final rejection of the misguided calls to leave our citizens to fend for themselves—and bold leadership into the future." By seeking to build his "bridge into the twenty-first century" with such a rhetorically confusing flourish, Clinton had managed to move his party in a new direction. And congressional Democrats generally went along with him once they recognized the political value in following his lead. As House Minority Leader Richard Gephardt remarked during the fall campaign, "We are all New Democrats now."

While Clinton and Dole headed their respective party tickets, they both had to contend with Ross Perot, who had again entered the presidential sweepstakes. This time, however, Perot was not the resounding outsider whose attack on George Bush had helped to alter the balance in Clinton's favor in 1992. Now, news about his quirky personality and occasionally authoritarian pronouncements lessened his appeal for many voters. Yet Perot had the funds to transmit his views on the deficit and taxes, as well as campaign finance reform, to a potentially huge audience via televised infomercials. Using that medium, he focused attention on a growing campaign scandal that directly involved White House efforts to pay for Clinton's very expensive television advertising and for the polling that Dick Morris had undertaken since the summer of 1995.

Perot was indeed on to something, helped by media reports of apparent violations or abuses of campaign finance laws originating from within the Clinton White House. As journalist Lars-Erik Nelson later pointed out, there were "the White House kaffeeklatsches for big donors, the huge sums donated to the Democratic Party by shadowy overseas Chinese contributors, the administration's blatant peddling of access to the President and of opportunities to be photographed in his company with few questions asked." Clinton, in dire need of campaign contributions, found all that work tiring. He complained to Morris: "I can't think. I can't act. I can't do anything but go to fund raisers and shake hands. You want me to issue executive orders; I can't focus on a thing but the next fund raiser. Hillary can't. Al can't—we're all getting sick and crazy because of it."

Crazy or not, the Clinton White House stayed busy, renting out the Lincoln Bedroom for a night to well-heeled donors. In addition, Clinton spent time in the Map Room and the Roosevelt Room greeting campaign contributors, of whom several had been involved in the transfer of overseas money to the DNC or had appeared to have had strong underworld associations. Clinton's insatiable need for money may also have been a prime reason that he shifted policy on a sensitive national security issue. He took from the State Department the authority to determine whether the transfer of satellite technology to China was in the national interest and gave it to the Commerce Department, which viewed such matters in terms of markets and trade. This, of course, made it far easier for several firms engaged with products having a potential military function to get the necessary clearance to make their various deals with Beijing. In that same vein, Clinton also granted a waiver to Bernard Schwartz, the CEO of Loral Space and Communications, that gave him the legal authority to send another satellite to China. Schwartz was the largest single campaign donor to the DNC in 1996. Such was his generosity that over the years he ultimately gave the party more than a million dollars, including $100,000 sent just four weeks before Clinton approved a waiver in early July 1996. Both parties to the arrangement thus got what they needed and desired.

Several elements of this money-centered story were not known until well after the election. But enough had been reported by October 1996 about illegal money flows from Asia to the DNC, as well as the subletting of the Lincoln Bedroom, to raise dark suspicions that the Clinton White House had handled its campaign finances in an unseemly and improper, if not illegal, manner. Both Dole and Perot stressed that point at a crucial juncture during the fall campaign, and their attacks, coming in the waning days before the election, evidently affected the outcome of some congressional races, much to the detriment of the Democrats, who earlier had the House of Representatives within reach.

Dole, meanwhile, was on the ropes, and many Republican officeholders, sensing what was going to happen, had long since separated themselves from his campaign to help ensure their chances of keeping control of Congress. While Dole's campaign failed to take off, Perot no longer had the same appeal that he had for many voters in 1992. Although Perot sought to raise serious issues in the campaign, his base of support had contracted considerably. Yet he still commanded attention with his televised infomericals, which probably drained some support from the Democrats on the eve of the election.

Although Clinton lost ground as a result of those attacks, he still held a very comfortable lead over his two opponents, which election day confirmed. With less than half of the voting-age population going to the polls, Clinton won just over 49 percent of the popular vote, while Dole received 41 percent and Perot 9 percent. Clinton's sweep in the Electoral College was impressive, winning 379 votes to Dole's 159. Indeed, Clinton had risen from the political dead, thanks to the assistance he had received from Dick Morris on one hand and Newt Gingrich on the other. Morris had provided the game plan for Clinton's reelection drive, and Gingrich and his Republican cohorts in Congress had given Clinton the opportunity to target them successfully as "extremist" in their views and programs.

The strong support Clinton also garnered from both college- and high school–educated women helps to explain why he made such a comeback. They appreciated his defense of family values and his support of gun control, safe neighborhoods, pro-choice abortion rights, and protection for key federal programs focusing on education and the environment. In addition, many working women had experienced a slight increase in their household income since mid-1995 and were now convinced that the economy was finally on the right track. For a combination of reasons, then, their very substantial vote for Clinton, amounting to 54 percent for him and only 38 percent for Dole, was instrumental in helping to create the margin by which he won reelection.

Democrats in Congress did not match Clinton's success. They fell short of capturing the House by several seats, even though it appeared that they were in a position to do so two weeks before the election. Dole and Perot, having focused on Clinton's campaign violations, drove some voters into the arms of the GOP at the last minute. In addition, corporate America, by outspending organized labor by a margin of seven to one, also put enough into the till to make a difference at the end. Furthermore, although the Democrats were competitive in many House races, Clinton gave them little help, seeing no good advantage for himself in doing so. Finally, the fact that only 46 percent of white males voted for Democratic House candidates in 1996 probably spelled the difference between victory and defeat in many close elections throughout the country.

As usual, big money played a key role in the unfolding political drama of that year. Most important was the unlimited amount of soft money a campaign donor could give to either the Democratic or Republican National Committee. Since that money was ostensibly used for the purpose of advancing a party agenda, not the election of a specific candidate, the Federal Election Commission deemed any such contribution proper and legal. Consequently, the Republican Party raised $138.2 million in soft money, while the Democrats took in $123.9 million. In the case of the Democrats, the White House controlled the contributions given to the DNC, which was used to pay for the issue advertising on television that Dick Morris had prepared. Because he was not constrained by the financial limits that applied to the Clinton–Gore campaign committee, Morris could spend what he thought was necessary for those ads without having to worry about objections coming from the Federal Election Commission.

Yet some of money that the DNC had funneled to the White House for Morris's activities was clearly tainted. It came from highly questionable foreign sources, including groups from Indonesia and China, which sought to gain access to and influence in the American political and governmental system for their own purposes. As a result, the operation and function of the DNC's money machine soon came under intense scrutiny and investigation by a congressional committee in the newly elected 105th Congress.

Weeks before that Congress came into session, both Clinton and Gingrich had talked about the need to find "common ground." Most likely, a top priority for each was the need to get a balanced budget agreement that would lessen the likelihood of another government shutdown, which earlier had proven to be so costly for the Republicans. Clinton also spoke about the need to restore the "Vital Center" in American politics. Precisely what he meant by this was not clear. Did it mean that he would seek to cooperate with Republicans to reform traditional Democratic entitlement programs such as Social Security and Medicare against the wishes of liberal Democrats in Congress? Or to support a balanced budget having more in common with the GOP's agenda than with his own congressional party?

As Clinton prepared to take the oath of office for a second time, his job approval rating stood at 60 percent, helped by a good economy, a substantially reduced deficit, astute centrist-driven politics, and a stable international environment. But as a serious student of the American presidency, Clinton was well aware that second-term troubles and major disasters had often enveloped earlier inhabitants of the office. Whether he could avoid a similar fate, at a time of intense partisanship, deep cultural division, and a pervasive feeling that government could do little or nothing to improve the lives of most citizens, was about to be tested.

Chapter Four

From the Center to the Edge

As Bill Clinton prepared to move into his second term as president, he appointed Madeleine Albright, the current U.S. representative to the United Nations, as secretary of state. Samuel Berger, assistant national security adviser, became his new national security adviser. Former Republican Senator William Cohen was selected as the new secretary of defense. Alexis Herman, a key White House aide, succeeded the departing Robert Reich as secretary of labor.

The next order of business for Clinton was the devising of an agenda to justify his second term. What was he to do now that he had co-opted a number of Republican issues such as crime and welfare? At the top of his list was reaching a balanced budget agreement with the GOP. Since Clinton had already committed himself to seek "common ground" with Speaker Newt Gingrich, it was only a matter of time before the two of them worked out their differences. Whether Clinton would push hard for new departures in public policy was more uncertain. He recognized that the economy was booming and a majority of Americans desired few major new initiatives from government. So Clinton was constrained from moving too rapidly in any new direction, especially because he was generally disinclined to do anything that ran counter to the polls. The good news was that his job approval rating stood at 60 percent in a New York Times/CBS News poll, which was his highest rating in four years in office, and compared favorably with Ronald Reagan's 62 percent at the beginning of his second term.

Having been sworn in for a second time, the president revealed nothing of his future intentions in his bland inaugural address other than to call for an end to "bickering and extreme partisanship." More to the point were his remarks in the State of the Union address, which he delivered on February 4, 1997. His "call to action" on that occasion included enlarging of the Head Start program to reach a million children by the year 2002, repairing the country's education system, and expanding NAFTA. Clinton's bite-size initiatives were in line with the goal of a balanced budget by the year 2002 and contrasted sharply with 1993, when he spoke out on behalf of higher taxes, a radical revamping of the health industry, and a request for $30 billion for highways and summer jobs.

Clinton's overall 1998 budget also reflected the new imperative. While seeking to reinstate the right of childless adults to collect food stamps if they were unemployed and could not find work, it capped federal spending per Medicaid enrollee. The basic element of Clinton's budget appeared to provide the basis for forging a budgetary compromise with the Republican Congress. With the GOP amenable to serious talks with the White House, both sides negotiated a budget deal, much to the consternation of many key House and Senate Democrats, who were left in the cold while those private discussions took place.

The booming American economy, which grew at a spectacular rate of 5.6 percent in the first quarter, was the key to making that compromise work, as it sent unexpected billions of tax dollars flowing into Treasury Department vaults. Thanks to that development, along with slower spending on Medicare and Medicaid programs, the projected federal deficit declined to $75 billion, thereby giving both sides the budgetary flexibility they needed to seal a final deal in late July 1997. The GOP got its tax cut, which included a reduction in the capital gains tax, a $500 per child tax credit for most families, and raising the ultimate estate exemption from federal taxes to over $1 million. Although this legislation was ostensibly designed to provide the middle class with tax relief, the top 1 percent of taxpayers, making more than $246,000 per annum, were the real beneficiaries. They received 68 percent of the total tax cut, amounting to $7,135 per individual, while those earning under $59,000 a year received an average cut of $6. At the same time, Clinton got an extra $24 billion, which included funds given to the states for health insurance for children from low-income working families. In addition, the legislation reinstated the welfare eligibility for legal immigrants who were denied such status as a result of the 1996 welfare act, and spending on food stamps was slightly increased.

Also significant were the spending cuts in key programs such as Medicare and Medicaid. Although the structure of those programs was kept intact, such cuts affected funds allocated to hospitals, doctors, and other health care providers, thereby creating added financial pressures on various medical institutions. And both sides agreed that monthly Medicare premiums had to be raised to help pay for the growing cost of that program.

Concurrently, very tight spending caps on future appropriations were included in the budget package, which, in the words of former Clinton Budget Director Leon Panetta, would require "drastic reductions in spending, totaling $775 billion over 10 years, with the first $25 billion cut due in fiscal year 2000." In time, however, both parties were to discover that those restrictive caps had played havoc with their respective political agendas and priorities. Thus, each party would later seek ways of circumventing a budget deal that many House Democrats, led by Minority Leader Richard Gephardt, had flatly opposed in 1997 on the grounds that it mainly benefited affluent Americans at the expense of middle-income earners and the working poor.

Despite Gephardt's opposition, Clinton and Gingrich celebrated. On August 5, 1997, they met in a spirit of bipartisanship at the White House ceremony for the signing of the Balanced Budget Act and the Taxpayer Relief Act. Yet their rhetorical lovefest did not alter the fact that many Republicans on Capitol Hill were eager to challenge Clinton wherever possible, which included putting a spotlight on recent multiple Democratic Party campaign finance abuses. Hence, the Senate authorized the Senate Governmental Affairs Committee, headed by Tennessee's Fred Thompson, to conduct "an investigation of illegal or improper activities in connection with the 1996 federal election campaigns." By following the money, Thompson's committee highlighted the flow of illegal or improper Asian and domestic financial contributions to the White House during the 1996 campaign. But the refusal of many potentially important witnesses to testify hampered the committee's investigation. Ten individuals fled the country, placing themselves beyond the reach of congressional subpoenas. Not surprisingly, the committee's final report was divided along partisan political lines. More important, despite the leads and evidence these hearings did produce, Attorney General Janet Reno refused to appoint independent counsels to pursue them, thereby protecting the Clinton administration from what otherwise might have been a crippling political scandal.

Although President Clinton was protected by the Reno Justice Department, he could not escape the scrutiny of the Supreme Court. In May 1997, it allowed the Paula Jones civil suit to proceed against him. If Clinton had made an effort to settle with Jones early in the process, he would have avoided prolonging a situation that eventually led to his impeachment. Meanwhile, he continued to receive high job approval ratings from the American public, mostly because of a flourishing economy and a stock market surge of historic proportions.

The economy was indeed moving along at high speed in 1997, averaging nearly 4 percent growth for the year. The Dow Jones industrial average flirted with 8,000. Unemployment dropped to 4.8 percent, which was the lowest figure in twenty-three years. And the wages of those at the bottom of the workforce were finally beginning to show slight improvement for the first time in years. More specifically, the steady gain in the stock market augmented consumer confidence and well-being, which in turn helped to drive the economy. Firms could afford to raise wages without having to increase prices on their goods, thanks to enhanced productivity growth that reached a remarkable 4.5 percent in the third quarter of 1997 and a measurable decline in unit labor costs. (As defined by *New York Times* business reporter Louis Uchitelle, "Productivity measures the value of what a worker produces in goods or services during an hour on the job.") Also contributing to the prevailing price stability was a flood of cheap imports from Asia, which forced many American firms to remain price competitive at home. As a result of these various factors, inflation was happily contained at a very low level in 1997, much to the relief of both Alan Greenspan and the Clinton administration.

Work was also plentiful, helped by the creation of over nineteen million new jobs in the 1990s. In the fast-changing blue-collar world, for example, many workers found decently paying jobs as skilled technicians of one sort or another. And unskilled black and Latino workers were being hired in growing numbers as a result of a tightening labor market. And while many of them benefited only marginally from a strong economy, they still had ample reason to believe, like so many others, that times were good and that Clinton was doing an excellent job of removing the thorns from the rose garden of prosperity. As Democratic pollster Peter Hart put it, "The American people are judging

President Clinton on what counts for them, and that's the economy. Americans' high paychecks translate into higher Clinton ratings."

While Clinton's political standing seemed secure for the moment, the growing economic disorder in Asia was casting its shadow over boom times in America. Beginning as a currency crisis in Thailand, it soon spread to other Asian economies such as South Korea, Hong Kong, Indonesia, and Singapore, and thereby threatened to destabilize the entire global economy. Deeply concerned about that possibility, the Clinton administration worked hard to find the resources, via the International Monetary Fund (IMF) and other lending institutions, to shore up and repair drastically weakened economic structures in desperate need of sudden short-term capital infusion. Operating with American blessings, it pushed an austerity-driven agenda requiring the closing of failing banks and businesses as well as massive job layoffs. And while these IMF "reforms" were being put in place, American investors were already moving in to pick up bankrupt Asian firms at bargain basement prices. As Jeffery Garten, a former Clinton administration undersecretary of commerce, remarked: "Most of these countries are going to go through a deep and dark tunnel. . . . But on the other end there is going to be a significantly different Asia in which Americans have achieved a much deeper market penetration, much greater access."

While the process of recovery and "reform" in Asia was under way, several countries, including South Korea, were forced to devalue their currencies, which made their export products even more competitive in American marketplace. That step exacerbated the already serious trade deficit the United States was running with Asia. As a result of the deep Asian recession, it also meant that American manufacturing firms and their employees, heavily dependent on the export market to Asia, would feel the pinch. But the underlying problem of the global economy was largely hidden from public view. The overcapacity of plant and production facilities, with too few consumers, was a potential threat to the economic stability of the industrial world at the end of the twentieth century.

Although the administration managed to force compliance upon weakened Asian economies heavily dependent on American and/or IMF bailouts for survival, the situation was very different with Congress. There, Clinton was in deep trouble as he sought fast-track authority (requiring an up-or-down vote in Congress on an entire proposal with no amendments allowed) to negotiate the extension of NAFTA southward to include Chile. Although the debate in the House was similar to the one held on NAFTA, this time the result was different. Clinton and important business groups had failed to enter the fight over fast-track authority until it was much too late to shape the final outcome; thus they lost. And so did high-tech managers, who wanted free access to world markets and no binding trade agreements that might include tighter environmental and labor standards for workers overseas. The key to the ultimate outcome was a full-scale mobilization undertaken by organized labor to ensure that living standards and the well-being of working Americans were protected from the ravages of the global economy. Fortunately for the AFL-CIO, many House Democrats agreed that future trade agreements had to include provisions protecting working conditions and the environment. Lacking the votes, Clinton withdrew his request for fast-track authority, thereby giving labor, in the words of John Sweeney, a "really big win."

Although Republicans, led by Speaker Gingrich, generally supported Clinton on fast-track legislation and had worked with him to balance the budget, the tenor of politics was still rife with intense partisanship in late 1997. GOP conservatives continued to push for additional tax cuts and school vouchers, while Democrats flatly opposed such measures, supporting instead added funding for education and health programs as well as campaign finance reform. Because both parties were already busily skirmishing and posturing on these and other issues well before the 1998 election, there was little chance that much significant new legislation would pass during the first session of the 105th Congress.

At the same time, several Democrats sought to initiate a serious discussion over the future direction of their party. In that vein, House Minority Leader Richard Gephardt, a possible candidate for the 2000 Democratic presidential nomination, pointedly remarked that "Too often, our leaders seem enamored with small ideas that nibble around the edges of big problems." Contrasting himself with the New Democrats in the White House, Gephardt was critical of policies coming from an administration that had embraced Republican-backed proposals from welfare to balanced budgets to tax cuts while it failed to do much for millions of workers who still suffered from wage stagnation. Vice President Al Gore, the leading flag-waver of Clintonism, quickly derided "the huffing and puffing of out-of-shape and out-of-date dogmas trying to keep up with the dynamism of the new economy."

While the remarks of Gephardt and Gore spoke to the deep divisions that separated the two wings of the Democratic Party, Clinton soon moved the debate in a different direction. On January 5, 1998, he announced that the projected deficit for 1998 would be under $22 billion and that his next federal budget would be balanced. A remarkable achievement coming three years ahead of time, it resulted from "a very strong economy, wise fiscal policy adopted in 1990 and 1993, enlightened monetary policy over the last seven years, and a substantial dash of good luck." In one fell swoop, the prospect of growing budget surpluses ended the era of the politics of deficits and austerity, which had shaped the political agenda of both parties for nearly two decades. Looking ahead, Republicans would argue for more tax cuts and paying down the federal debt. Democrats would seek to spend billions for "investments" in education, welfare, and Medicare. And both parties would begin to discuss and debate how best to preserve the viability of the Social Security trust fund for the future retirees of the baby boom generation.

In the meantime, Clinton sought to repair the damage caused by the defection of so many Democrats during the struggle over fast-track legislation, which, in some cases, occurred because of their personal dislike for him. Moving back to a policy-oriented agenda favored by many liberal Democrats, he embraced several initiatives such as a multibillion-dollar child care program, greater funding for education, and plans to let the near-elderly buy into Medicare. House Minority Whip David Bonior was pleased with this move, and thought that Clinton's legislative agenda "will make him more in sync with us and us with him." As this new rapprochement was beginning to take hold between Clinton and the House Democratic caucus, the *Wall Street Journal*'s Paul Gigot shrewdly observed that a government that "lives within its means" is "one the public may be willing to trust with more ways and means."

But whether the Democrats could benefit politically from the emergence of "balanced budget liberalism" was yet to be determined. In the meantime, a totally unforeseen development changed the flow of events in a dramatic way. The media, led by the Internet's *Drudge Report*, revealed on January 20–21, 1998, that Clinton had had an on-going sexual relationship with Monica Lewinsky, a White House intern. This news stunned the nation, leaving many citizens dismayed and disgusted with Clinton's behavior. Subsequently, Clinton had

Dick Morris poll citizens about the matter, and he, in turn, reported that the country would tolerate a presidential affair but not perjury or an obstruction of justice. Several days later, Clinton appeared on television and denied having had "sexual relations with that woman, Miss Lewinsky" and added that he had never instructed anyone to lie, "not a single time—never."

But complicating matters for Clinton was not just the matter of his public mendacity. In his January 17, 1998, deposition filed in the Paula Jones civil case, he denied having had a sexual relationship with Lewinsky. Earlier, Lewinsky had submitted an affidavit in the Jones case, declaring that she did not have a sexual relationship with the president. Thus, the two of them had not only left themselves open to charge of perjury. Clinton may also have hinted to Lewinsky to file a false affidavit in order to avoid being deposed, which meant that there was the added possibility that he had obstructed justice as well.

Such potentially serious legal charges resulted from crucial evidence supplied to the Office of Independent Counsel by Linda Tripp, a confidante of Lewinsky's, who had taped conversations that spelled out the extent of her affair with Clinton. Not only did those tapes confirm that Lewinsky had lied in her affidavit, but they provided Kenneth Starr's office, originally charged to investigate Whitewater, with possible leads into questionable White House activities that included Clinton's likely efforts to obstruct justice. Consequently, Starr sought to broaden his investigation of Whitewater to include the Lewinsky affair. Once presented with new material and questions needing answers, Attorney General Janet Reno recommended to a three-judge federal panel that the independent counsel be given the added authority. Permission was quickly granted. Thus, as a result of Clinton's effort to cover up a series of sexual encounters with Lewinsky, which began in November 1995 and ended in late March 1997, he had moved from widespread popularity and domination of the political center to the edge of a possibly humiliating impeachment inquiry.

Seeking to save his presidency, Clinton delivered the State of the Union address on January 27, 1998, in which he announced that the United States now had "the smallest government in thirty-five years, but a more progressive one." He also declared that he was submitting a balanced budget to Congress for the next fiscal year and stated that projected surpluses to come should be used to "Save Social Security first." Then pushing modestly in the direction of what the *New York Times* defined as "Progressivism lite," he called for an increase in the minimum wage, the hiring of 100,000 new teachers, a major initiative on child care, and more funding for biomedical and scientific research. More important than the content of his speech was the fact that Clinton had showed himself to be in complete control, giving no sign that his dalliance with Lewinsky had affected his capacity to govern or lead.

In addition, Clinton was helped by the strong endorsement he received in the polls following his State of the Union address. His job approval rating jumped from 57 percent to 73 percent, and the polls revealed that a majority of Americans believed that his affair with Lewinsky was a purely private and personal matter. A similar majority also believed that even if he had behaved unethically, he could still perform his presidential duties with integrity. Most revealing only 26 percent believed that Kenneth Starr was "mainly interested in conducting a fair and impartial investigation," while 57 percent thought otherwise. These polling figures, working to Clinton's advantage, were to remain fairly constant throughout much of 1998, thereby indicating that he retained strong public support, especially with women and minorities, despite the growing efforts of a militant minority eager to remove him from office.

Although Clinton was beginning to win the battle in the court of public opinion, Starr was faced with a major decision that affected the future course of his investigation. Given an opportunity in early February 1998 to provide Lewinsky with a grant of immunity for her testimony, he refused to approve the grant of immunity that aides in the prosecutor's office had negotiated with her and her lawyer. Instead he sided with others in his office who first wanted a face-to-face interview with Lewinsky before extending to her such a grant, a stance which immediately nullified the earlier agreement. Starr's decision resulted in a delay of five months before he finally gave Lewinsky immunity for her testimony. His failure to grant her immunity in February may have cost him valuable time to make a much stronger legal case against the president, before the White House could fully mobilize a well-directed counterattack, accusing him of launching a politically motivated vendetta.

While the Lewinsky scandal absorbed the attention of the country thanks in large part to intense media coverage, serious consideration of other issues seemed, for the moment, relegated to the back burner. As historian Garry Wills wrote, "There are no great debates on great issues. Party loyalty is down, voter apathy up. The vacuum in political interest is filled more and more by obsession with headline trials." Wills's point was well taken: the country's preoccupation with private gain and public spectacles, such as the O. J. Simpson trial (1995), bespoke a general placidity in the public realm that a very good economy and the ending of the Cold War had helped to create. In that regard former Labor Secretary Robert Reich put it best: Americans preferred "to compare stock portfolios, banter about culture and identity and tut-tut over problems decades hence, like an insolvent Social Security trust fund or excessive greenhouse gases."

Despite that omnipresent complacency, the country was not lacking in important issues, whether at home or abroad. Millions of working Americans still did not benefit from the great boom of the 1990s, as they continued to suffer from the blight of wage stagnation, which left many with less purchasing power in 1998 than in 1989. And 20 percent of American children lived in a state of poverty. At least forty million Americans lacked health insurance, while many others who had coverage were often at the mercy of uncaring and insensitive health maintenance organizations. So despite the phenomenal growth in the availability of new jobs, corporate downsizing and mass layoffs remained a sad fact of life and a constant source of anxiety for a mostly nonunionized workforce rightly fearing the impact of those cost-cutting measures.

Also, very few observers publicly noticed that the boom of the 1990s was driven to a considerable extent by an enormous expansion of corporate and consumer debt. For example, although the ratio of household debt to after-tax income stood at 59 percent in 1984, it reached 83 percent in 1997. Furthermore, the ratio of bank loans to deposits in 1997 had climbed to a record high of 88 percent, while total household debt reached $5.5 trillion. Not surprisingly, then, an average of 17 percent of disposable household income now went to service debt, which, according to the *New York Times*, also included an average payment of $1,000 a year in credit card interest and fees. Given that level of corporate and personal debt, a sudden economic downturn or a deep and prolonged recession could readily undermine the financial well-being of millions of people lacking the resources to pay the interest on their debt load, thereby driving down the consumer consumption on which overall prosperity depended.

Because these domestic matters failed to ignite public outrage or concern, Clinton was not about leave the safe moorings of the political center to deal with them, especially while he was preoccupied with the fallout from the Lewinsky affair. Yet troubled as he was at home, Clinton could not ignore developments elsewhere, such as the continuing economic crisis in Asia and current relations with China and Russia, which intersected with America's global strategic and economic interests. Shaken by the Asian recession, which had the potential to unravel the global economy, he urged Congress to give the IMF a fresh $18 billion to cope with future crises. Although his request was delayed because of strong opposition in Congress from conservatives and liberals alike, fortunately for all concerned, including several important American banks, a number of Asian economies began to recover from their bout of the financial flu by midsummer of 1998.

Constructive engagement with China also remained a key component of American policy in Asia. Pursuant to that objective, President Clinton sought to forge a viable relationship based on trade and mutual cooperation on issues of common concern. By relaxing rules governing the shipment of sensitive satellite technology and supercomputers to China, Clinton had eased the way for leading Chinese officials visiting the White House in 1997 and 1998. His goal was to gain their support in halting the shipment of nuclear technology to Iran and missile technology to Pakistan. In late June 1998, Clinton, having defended his policy as "principled and pragmatic," went to Beijing, where he discussed the common interests the two sides shared and publicly decried the Tiananmen Square massacre of June 1989. Although the American people thought Clinton's visit was both necessary and successful, continuing Chinese human rights violations, mounting evidence of an infusion of Chinese money in the 1996 presidential election, and a burgeoning American trade deficit with China worried many in Congress. Despite growing criticism of the administration's policies, Congress voted to continue China's most-favored-nation status and treatment inside the American market.

In the spring of 1998, Clinton also sought the Senate's endorsement of his proposal to extend NATO in an eastward direction to include Poland, the Czech Republic, and Hungary. In a letter to members of the Senate, he said that such a move "would help to erase the Cold War dividing line and contribute to our strategic goal of building an undivided, democratic and peaceful Europe." But Democratic Senator Dale Bumpers feared the possible risks that this initiative might pose to the future of Russo-American relations, stating that "NATO expansion is designed to hem Russia in." Republican Senator John Warner wondered about the need to expand NATO in the first place, asking "what will it do, what is its mission?" And the *New York Times* called Clinton's proposed expansion of NATO a "gratuitous risk" that could threaten the stability of Europe. It feared that given Russia's "volatile political environment" this "expansion could easily be exploited by nationalist forces intent on diminishing democracy and chilling relations with the West." The Senate, ignoring the *Times* analysis, voted 80 to 19 to approve Clinton's request, which delighted many defense contractors, who had campaigned hard on Capitol Hill for the measure in anticipation of securing new markets in Eastern Europe for their various lethal products. As foreign policy specialist William G. Hyland observed, "building European security without, or against, Russia has not worked for four centuries."

Whatever serious trouble NATO's expansion might yet create for the United States lay in the future. More immediately worrisome for the Clinton administration was the near-total collapse of the Russian economy. On August 17, 1998, Moscow gave notice that it was devaluing the ruble, defaulting on its own short-term treasury bills, and imposing a moratorium on bank-held loans. That action caused shock waves to ripple through the global economy and forced the IMF and the World Bank to shelve a $17 billion aid package they were planning to send to Russia as long as a set of stringent economic conditions continued to be implemented.

Meanwhile, the $4.8 billion that the IMF had earlier sent to Russia to stabilize the ruble quickly disappeared from sight, raising deep suspicions about who controlled the disbursement of those funds. The vaporizing of that loan was symptomatic of the vast political and economic corruption inside Russia itself, which the Clinton administration had generally ignored. It was more concerned with whether the Duma would ratify the START II disarmament treaty and with whether Boris Yeltsin's regime would continue to pursue economic reform according to American rules and design.

Few Americans cared about these events in Russia. But many were "variously entertained and appalled and titillated" by Clinton's affair with Monica Lewinsky. For Clinton, it was not entertainment, however; Lewinsky had become a serious legal problem, especially after he had been subpoenaed by Kenneth Starr to present testimony about the affair. Although the subpoena was later withdrawn, Clinton voluntarily testified at the White House on August 17, 1998, which, coincidentally, was the same day Moscow announced that it had devalued the ruble and defaulted on its debt.

Even before Clinton underwent more than four hours of interrogation by representatives from Starr's office, he knew, as did the public, that Lewinsky had received a grant of immunity for her testimony, which she gave several weeks earlier. In his own testimony, which was fed to a federal grand jury via a television hookup, Clinton admitted to having an "inappropriate" relationship with Lewinsky that involved "intimate contact" of a sexual nature. But he denied having lied about it in his deposition in the Jones case, and he also refused to answer several questions that were directed at him.

That same night, Clinton, appearing uncontrite and angry, spoke on national television and gave slightly more than a four-minute address in which he finally publicly admitted, "I did have a relationship with Ms. Lewinsky that was not appropriate. . . . It constituted a critical lapse in judgment and a personal failure on my part for which I am solely and completely responsible." Having offered something considerably short of an apology for his previous lies and misrepresentations, he then proceeded to lash out at Starr's investigation, stating that it "has gone on too long, cost too much, and hurt too many innocent people." It was now time to move on, said Clinton, and "repair the fabric of our national discourse."

The tenor and content of Clinton's speech instantly galvanized a strong backlash against him in several newspapers across the country. The *Charleston* (West Virginia) *Daily Mail* delivered a sharp editorial rebuke: "In a ghastly four-minute session, the President told the nation no more than he had to. It was a calculated, carefully calibrated effort at damage control. It was a hell of a comedown from a fireside chat with F.D.R." And the *Detroit Free Press* opined that Clinton's "mantra of taking personal responsibility rings hollow. He has let the whole country down."

But despite that editorial onslaught, Clinton's high job approved rating in the polls dipped only slightly as a result of his address of August 17,

1998. And though Clinton's personal unfavorable rating rose from 33 percent to 40 percent, working in his favor were the feelings of a strong majority that his affair with Lewinsky was private in nature and that the investigation should be dropped. At the same time, only 19 percent viewed Kenneth Starr favorably, while 43 percent did not.

Starr had clearly lost the public relations battle with Clinton, but he still was obligated by statute to submit a report to Congress about his findings. Consequently, on September 9, 1998, he sent to the House a referral containing "substantial and credible information that President William Jefferson Clinton committed acts that may constitute grounds for impeachment." It alleged that Clinton had lied under oath at a civil deposition; had lied under oath to a grand jury; had "attempted to obstruct justice by facilitating a witness's plan to refuse to comply with a subpoena"; and had "engaged in a pattern of conduct that was inconsistent with his constitutional duty to faithfully execute the laws."

The Republican-controlled House released Starr's report two days later, and it was immediately disseminated to the public via the Internet and other media outlets, shocking many readers with its graphic and detailed account of Clinton's sexual encounters with Lewinsky. White House lawyers quickly sought to rebut Starr's report by stating that in the Constitution "high crimes and misdemeanors" meant "wrongs committed against our system of government" and that impeachment "was never designed to allow a political body to force a President from office for a very personal mistake."

As the battle lines formed between Starr's supporters and many detractors, the Republican-controlled House Judiciary Committee voted to release a video of Clinton's four-hour interrogation of August 17, hoping that it would give them added support in moving against him. But contrary to Republican hopes, that video changed few minds: a New York Times/CBS News poll revealed that a firm majority, though strongly disapproving of Clinton's behavior, did not want him removed from office, nor did they want him to resign. They believed that he was an effective leader who was doing a good job as president, and only by a narrow margin did they favor a punishment, such as a censure resolution, that fell far short of the impeachment resolution some Republicans clearly wanted. Having already viewed Starr's investigation and his report as a mostly partisan effort to damage the president, the public felt the same about the release of the video.

The good economy that prevailed everywhere protected Clinton from large-scale voter dissatisfaction with his leadership. As a Republican from upstate New York put it:

This country seems to be doing very well, and I don't see that a personal problem has anything to do with running the country. The stock market is doing very well. There are more jobs for people. Basically, I think that the American people are happier than they have been in many years.

Such, however, was not the case inside the beltway. There, Democrats, having to face the electorate in November, worried about the impact of Clinton's affair on their prospects. And recent poll data notwithstanding, the Republican House leadership was prepared to move against him in order to satisfy its conservative base, whose support it needed for money and votes in the upcoming midterm election. With Gingrich controlling the agenda, the House voted on October 8, largely along party lines, to uphold the Judiciary Committee's earlier decision to proceed with an impeachment inquiry. By rejecting a Democratic proposal to limit the inquiry, the Republicans had thus left themselves wide open to the charge that they were unfairly pursuing the president.

As the fall election approached, with so much at stake for all sides, Bill Clinton announced on September 30 that the government had reached the end of the current fiscal year with a $70 billion budget surplus—the first surplus since 1969, and the largest in history. Clinton wanted it used to bolster the Social Security trust fund for the retirees of the baby boom generation, whereas Republicans believed that it provided an opportunity for another big tax cut.

With the surplus serving as a backdrop to talks designed to end another deadlock over the budget, Clinton, politically nimble and ever resourceful even while facing an impeachment inquiry, outmaneuvered the Republicans once more. At the conclusion of eight days of talks, he obtained a budget deal that was a major political triumph for himself and the Democrats and a defeat for Gingrich and his fellow negotiators. Because Gingrich feared another government shutdown, at a time when Republicans were eager to leave town and start campaigning, he was forced to give way on many key issues. Thus, Clinton, largely driving the terms of the $500 billion budget deal, won from Republicans $18 billion for the IMF, an increase in spending to combat global warming, and $1.1 billion to help school districts hire 100,000 elementary school teachers. At the same time, he agreed to add $9 billion more to the military budget, raising it to close to $280 billion, which was the biggest single increase the Pentagon had received since the Gulf War. Finally, both sides agreed to create an additional $20 billion package to cover "emergencies."

Although Clinton appeared in a weakened state, his remarkable performance during the budget negotiations won him praise from Democrats, who were delighted that he had headed off major Republican tax cut proposals. Republican conservatives denounced Gingrich for having given away the shop. Much to their dismay and disgust, they saw their fading hopes for a serious tax cut dashed by this agreement. Gingrich, calling his conservative critics "perfectionists," defended the deal, saying that it was the best that could be achieved "when you have a conservative Republican Congress and a liberal Democratic President." The good news was that he had avoided another government shutdown, but there was little else for him to show for a year's work. Deadlock over substantive policy issues was the norm of government at this point, as neither party had the means to fully prevail under current political circumstances, preventing the passage of significant legislation in either political direction. Given that reality, the 105th Congress finished its work and went home to await the results of the November 3, 1998, election, whose outcome might yet determine the fate of the House impeachment inquiry.

Gingrich, desperate to increase the narrow Republican majority in the House, predicted that his party would win anywhere from ten to forty new seats as a result of the Clinton scandal. Senate Republicans talked about achieving enough victories to assure them of sixty seats, allowing them, say, to terminate Democratic filibusters on measures they wanted passed. Democrats, in the meantime, were hopeful of containing their losses thanks to Clinton's finessing of the budget deal, while they concentrated on issues that would bring their key supporters to the voting booth.

The results were quite unexpected: the election of five more Democrats to the House ended Republican hopes that the president's scandal was their ticket to a big victory. Instead, the Republicans were left with the slimmest possible control of the House in the upcoming 106th Congress. And the ratio in the Senate remained as before, with the Republicans retaining fifty-five seats to forty-five for the Democrats. Clearly, the GOP, running solely against Clinton, had failed to give voters other reasons to vote for it. Unlike 1994, when it had campaigned on the Contract with America, the party now lacked both an agenda and a direction to overcome those deep ideological divisions in its own ranks. In fact, some conservatives were so angry at Gingrich for his failure to deliver in the budget talks and his lack of success in passing their agenda that they voted for moderate Democratic candidates opposed to abortion. On the other hand, some Republican women voted for Democratic candidates because they disliked Gingrich and his impeachment strategy.

A more detailed look at the 1998 election also revealed that a mere 36.1 percent of eligible voters had gone to the polls, which was the lowest turnout for a midterm election since 1942. Yet the Democrats were able to win five more House seats, which was the first time since 1934 that the party controlling the White House increased its numbers in Congress in a midterm election. Labor's role was particularly important in that it mobilized Democrats at the grass roots to turn out and vote, which was not the case in 1996 when it had devoted its political budget to television advertising.

While Democrats reveled in the defeat of New York Senator Al D'Amato and Gray Davis's victory as governor of California, the reality was that the GOP still controlled Congress and a majority of stathouses. Most significantly, George W. Bush, the son of former President George Bush, won reelection as governor of Texas with a massive 69 percent of the vote. The magnitude of his triumph, in a state with the third highest number of electoral votes, immediately catapulted him into the position of likely front-runner for the presidential nomination of the Republican Party in 2000.

Unlike Governor Bush, who appeared to have a bright future, Speaker Gingrich's best days were behind him. Three days after the election, he stunned the political world by announcing that he was resigning his position and would leave Congress altogether in January. Harshly criticized by members of his caucus for his handling of the budget negotiations and his campaign strategy of focusing on Clinton at the expense of socially conservative ideas, Gingrich knew that he faced a serious challenge to his leadership position in the 106th Congress. It was a situation full of irony. After many years of wandering in the desert, he had led the Republicans into the promised land of a majority in the House as the chief spokesman and fomenter of the Republican revolution. But his grating style and partisan manner made him the Democrats' favorite target of abuse, while many conservatives felt that he was never really one of them. Although he sought to mollify the conservative firebrands in his own caucus, he had also worked with Clinton to get legislation such as NAFTA through the House. Gingrich's resignation thus deprived Democrats of a political personality and symbol that voters had come to dislike as much as they did.

In the meantime, the White House was much relieved by the results of the 1998 election. It thought that the Democratic comeback, along with voter disapproval of the impeachment inquiry, had shelved the prospect that the House, in a lame-duck session, would actually vote to impeach the president. That is why it wanted to expedite the committee's hearings, in the belief that Democrats and moderate Republicans working together would block any such move.

Clinton soon moved on another front in the struggle to hold his office. On November 13, 1998, he agreed to pay Paula Jones $850,000 to end her lawsuit against him without having to apologize and admit wrongdoing. This he did out of fear that Jones might win her appeal to a circuit court to have her case reinstated after it had been dismissed earlier in April by federal Judge Susan Webber Wright. (Judge Wright had ruled that Jones had not offered "tangible" evidence of a damaged career because of her confrontation with Clinton.) While seeking to reassure House Democrats that he had nothing else to hide, and worried that his admission of guilt in the Lewinsky affair might have strengthened the Jones appeal, Clinton settled the matter. If he had only acted years earlier, there would have been no trial where Lewinsky's name surfaced in a manner that exposed her and the president to public scrutiny from Kenneth Starr's investigation.

With the Jones case behind him, Clinton and his advisers still had to deal with the situation in the House, where they remained hopeful of avoiding impeachment. Their optimism was misplaced, largely because Tom DeLay, the powerful Republican Majority Whip, was willing to push for a floor vote for the impeachment that he strongly desired. Since the Republican members of the Judiciary Committee, led by Chairman Henry Hyde, shared DeLay's objective, Clinton was not home free. For them the case against Clinton was partly a matter of conviction as well as the need for money and votes, which required that they play to their conservative base to help preserve a Republican majority in the House.

Most moral conservatives, including members of the religious right and intellectuals such as former Reagan Cabinet member

William Bennett, viewed Clinton through the prism of the cultural wars. They saw him as someone at the pinnacle of power whose sexual behavior and social policies had contributed to the continuing moral corruption and decay of the country. On the other side were those who defended Clinton because of his tolerance toward gays and his policies of support for women and racial minorities. Along with many others, they agreed that no matter how reckless and irresponsible Clinton had been, the scandal itself was about sex and privacy and did not warrant impeachment.

Also separating and polarizing the two sides were deeper considerations that federal Judge Richard Posner saw stemming from "unbridgeable differences in values that have their origin in temperament, upbringing, and life experiences rather than in reasoning to divergent conclusions from shared premises." Here then is a sound explanation as to why this debate had taken on such virulent overtones for both sides caught up in the impeachment drama.

Was Clinton's dalliance only about sex, as some of his supporters and opponents had argued? Philip Elman, a Washington lawyer with roots in past Democratic administrations, viewed the matter differently. He wrote that "The sex was little but the lies were big. As was his [Clinton's] disrespect for, and damage to, the rule of law and a judicial process which depends for its effective functioning upon truthful testimony of witnesses." The Republicans on the House Judiciary Committee sought to make their case against the president on precisely those grounds. After rejecting a very tough Democratic censure resolution condemning Clinton's behavior, which a majority of Americans vastly preferred to an impeachment resolution, the Judiciary Committee passed four articles of impeachment on a straight party-line vote. They included perjury, obstruction of justice, and the abuse of power. And as a result of the committee's action, the House was brought face to face for only the second time in American history with the need to vote on articles of impeachment directed at a president of the United States.

The Democrats had also prepared a strongly worded censure resolution for floor consideration as an alternative to impeachment, which some moderate Republicans were willing to support in numbers sufficient to command a likely majority. But Republican officials warned them that if they joined the Democrats in sponsoring such a resolution, they would face serious opposition in Republican primaries by supporters of the conservative right, who would surely have the backing and funds to challenge them. Understandably fearing that retribution, most moderates backed off from supporting it. Hence, Tom DeLay's strategy of avoiding a vote on censure now meant that impeachment had become the vehicle by which most Republicans expressed their implacable hostility to Clinton, whom (like many House Democrats) they never liked or trusted.

On December 19, as the House convened to deal with those articles, it was stunned by the sudden resignation of Speaker-designate Robert Livingston, whose own extramarital affairs were about to become public knowledge. Forced out by his own colleagues, Livingston went to the House floor and announced his resignation, adding that he was also leaving Congress in January, after declaring that "I must set the example that I hope President Clinton will follow." Thus, the politics of scandal had claimed a fresh victim.

Following Livingston's extraordinary announcement, the House confronted articles of impeachment. With emotions running very high on both sides of the aisle, it voted to approve two of the four articles. They were Article One, which charged the president with having committed perjury before a federal grand jury (228–206), and Article Three, which dealt with Clinton's obstruction of justice in the Paula Jones case (221–212). Rejected were Article Two, which stated that Clinton was guilty of perjury in the Paula Jones case, and Article Four, which charged him with an abuse of power resulting from his having given "perjurious, false and misleading sworn statements" to several questions contained in a Judiciary Committee questionnaire. As a consequence of those specific votes on Articles One and Three, Clinton became the first duly elected president ever to be impeached by the House of Representatives.

Later that same day many House Democrats joined Clinton in the Rose Garden to show solidarity with him, not because they liked or respected him but because they did not believe that the impeachment proceedings were warranted and because they "were scared to death of the Constitutional implications." With supportive Democrats gathered around him, Clinton remarked that "I have accepted responsibility for what I did wrong in my personal life, and I have invited members of Congress to work with us to find a reasonable bipartisan and proportionate response. That approach was rejected today by Republicans in the House, but I hope it will be embraced by the Senate."

Clinton's fate was now in the hands of the Senate. But given the results of the November election, which saw the Democrats holding on to their forty-five seats, it was highly unlikely that either article of impeachment would receive the necessary two-thirds majority to remove him from office. Nevertheless, as prescribed by the Constitution, a Senate trial to hear the House charges was scheduled to begin early in the newly convened 106th Congress. Meanwhile, with the economy booming, Clinton's job approval rating had jumped to 73 percent. As a result of the House's action, the GOP's approval rating had plunged into the 30s, its lowest point in several years.

Senator Trent Lott, the Senate Majority Leader, was well aware of the political price his party had paid for impeaching the president. For that reason, he was eager to expedite the Senate trial as quickly as possible in order to cut those losses. His hope of having a quick up-and-down vote on Clinton's guilt—knowing that the president would not be removed from office—was dashed by the determined effort of many conservative Republicans in the Senate, along with House Republicans, to run a full-scale trial based on the House articles of impeachment.

Consequently, a Senate trial began on January 7, 1999, opening the way for Chairman Hyde and other members of the House Judiciary Committee to present their case against the president, who himself was ably defended by skilled trial lawyers from the White House. After a thirty-seven days of trial full of lawyerly give and take, which deviated little from what was already known and argued during the House hearings, the Senate voted on the two articles on February 12, 1999. Although the ultimate outcome was never in doubt, the vote revealed how little support impeachment had in the Senate. The Senate rejected Article One, focusing on perjury, by 55 to 45, as 10 Republicans joined 45 Democrats to defeat it. With a tie vote of 50 to 50, the Senate also rejected the charge of obstruction of justice; and in this case 5 Republicans lined up with 45 Democrats to deny the House managers even a majority, much less the 67 they needed for a conviction. Subsequently, Democratic Senator Dianne Feinstein introduced a toughly worded censure resolution but it failed to get the necessary two-thirds vote needed to bring it to the floor of the Senate. Her failure to obtain passage of that resolution thus ended a constitutional saga about a matter that had divided and consumed the nation for over a year.

Immediately after the Senate trial ended, Clinton publicly declared that he was "profoundly sorry . . . for what I said and did to trigger these events and the great burden they have imposed on the Congress and the American people." Adding to Clinton's own personal burden, however, was the decision of Judge Susan Webber Wright, several months later, to fine him $90,000 for having giving false testimony in the Paula Jones case. He had, in her words, deliberately "undermined the integrity of the judicial system."

Legal reporter Jeffrey Toobin defended Clinton, seeing him as a victim of "extremists of the political right who tried to use the legal system to undo elections—in particular the two that put Bill Clinton in the White House." However accurate that statement may be on one level, there remains a deeper and more complex reality, which was captured by journalist Elizabeth Drew. She observed that

> The zealousness of the House managers didn't cancel out Clinton's deeds. Many uncommitted people, and even some of those who defended him publicly, thought that whatever the details and tortured explanations, Clinton was guilty in the overall sense, but that ejecting him from office was a disproportionate response.

As a fair and balanced appraisal of a sleazy drama totally lacking in heroes, it did not satisfy the extremist views on either side, but it did express a point of view shared by a majority of Americans who opposed the impeachment of the president.

Forever tarnished by this sad episode, Clinton later declared that he would wear his impeachment as a "badge of honor." Historian Joseph Ellis saw matters differently, however, contending that Monica Lewinsky is "a tin can that's tied to Clinton's tail that will rattle through the ages and through the pages of history books." For Clinton, who was deeply concerned with his legacy and ultimate historical standing, this was indeed a damning indictment, one which he would seek to overcome during his final two years in office.

Chapter Five

Seeking a Legacy

When Bill Clinton delivered the State of the Union address to Congress on January 19, 1999, his impeachment trial was still under way in the Senate. Yet he spoke with remarkable poise and concentration. Focusing on the need to protect the Social Security trust fund, he offered a plan for using 62 percent of a projected $4.4 trillion federal budget surplus over the next fifteen years to ensure the fund's solvency. He recommended that 11 percent of the surplus be set aside to allow individuals to invest in a pension scheme of their choosing while receiving funds "to match a portion of their savings." He also proposed that workers continue to receive full benefits even if they continued to work past the designated retirement age of sixty-five. Clinton contended that his financial plan was fiscally sound and that it would help reduce the publicly held federal debt of $3.7 trillion to a level not seen since World War I. In addition to protecting Social Security and Medicare for future retirees, Clinton's plan was also shrewdly designed to head off a Republican effort to push through Congress a major new tax cut, which was the common ideological denominator of all factions within the GOP.

Clinton's $1.8 trillion budget, submitted to Congress on February 7, 1999, spelled out the details of his spending priorities for fiscal year 1999–2000. It included an extra $17 billion for discretionary programs, such as the popular Head Start program, which had been expanded to include more children. A $1.3 billion, five-year program reinstated Medicaid and food stamp benefits for legal immigrants who came to the United States after Clinton had signed the welfare bill in August

1996. At the same time, he gave the military a $12 billion supplement to the $265 billion it had already received in fiscal year 1998.

Republicans challenged Clinton's agenda by calling for a big tax cut that would amount to nearly $800 billion over the next decade. They also favored an increase in military spending of $18.2 billion and the bolstering of Social Security by allowing recipients to open private accounts financed by the payroll tax itself. Despite recommending more federal funding for education, Republicans wanted to adhere to the tight spending caps contained in the 1997 budget agreement, which would force significant budgetary cuts in many programs such as the environment, science, and agriculture.

Although the Republican agenda eschewed the stark antigovernment themes of the Gingrich era, it featured major differences with the White House on spending priorities, ruling out an early deal. Nevertheless, the two sides had moved into a new era of growing budget surpluses, which changed the debate from one of deficits and balanced budgets to one that reflected real disagreement about to how best to improve the long-term financial integrity of Social Security and Medicare.

While Clinton sparred with the GOP about budgetary matters, impeachment proceedings had solidified his relationship with many House Democrats whose support he earlier had disdained. Working together, they were now increasingly unified around common goals, while attempting to protect the Clinton presidency from the Republican onslaught and to advance shared policy objectives. That convergence in views and programs had been under way just as the news of the Lewinsky affair became public knowledge. Now, with less than two years left in his presidency, Clinton was determined to make up for lost time in order to lay the groundwork for something more substantial than simply deflecting or co-opting Newt Gingrich's policies.

As the annual budget battle began to heat up in Congress, foreign policy concerns created unexpected distractions. Relations between Washington and Belgrade reached a dead end over developments in the Serbian province of Kosovo. There, tensions had grown as a result of Serbian President Slobodan Milosevic's effort to supress an insurgent movement for independence led by the Kosovo Liberation Army (KLA), which he branded a terrorist organization seeking to separate Kosovo from Serbia. Yet it was Serbia's ruthless and repressive domination of Albanian Kosovars, which had opened the door to the emergence and growth of the KLA.

As violence escalated on both sides, the United States and its NATO partners, mindful of what had already occurred in Bosnia and worried that the situation in Kosovo could ignite a wider war in the Balkans, hoped to find a diplomatic solution and to avoid direct military intervention in Kosovo. Clinton sent Richard Holbrooke to Belgrade in October 1998 to work out an arrangement with Milosevic, calling for the withdrawal of the bulk of Serb troops in Kosovo and the introduction of observers to monitor the situation on the ground in Kosovo. Although Milosevic appeared unfazed by the threat of military action, he generally complied with the terms Holbrooke sought.

The situation in Kosovo was extremely fluid, however, and the agreement tenuous at best. As the KLA stepped up its attack on Serbian forces still remaining in Kosovo, Belgrade responded with predictable brutality of its own. Most shocking in that regard was the murder of forty-five Kosovar civilians at Racak by Serb-led forces, which galvanized Secretary of State Madeleine Albright and other administration officials to seek a military answer to the problem of growing violence in Kosovo. While meeting with other top-level administration officials at the White House on January 19, 1999, she presented a plan for a "humanitarian intervention" in Kosovo, which called for access for NATO troops throughout Yugoslavia and autonomy for Kosovo.

Although President Clinton endorsed Albright's goals for any future talks with Milosevic, he had no intention of sending ground troops to Kosovo, since the Pentagon and many members of Congress strongly opposed any such move. Instead, Clinton opted to use air power. After Prime Minister Tony Blair of Great Britain and other NATO officials endorsed his approach, Clinton awaited the outcome of negotiations at Rambouillet, a castle outside Paris, where representatives from Belgrade and the KLA were scheduled to meet with American officials in an attempt to resolve the conflict.

That meeting ended in failure, as Milosevic's representatives rejected Washington's terms. In order to obtain the KLA's endorsement, Albright agreed to a referendum on independence for Kosovo after three years of autonomy. Milosevic did not believe that the military threat he faced in Kosovo was very serious, so he resisted the deal. It now seemed that hostilities between NATO forces and Serbia could no longer be avoided.

President Clinton did not seek a United Nations authorization for his contemplated military action, fearing a likely Russian or Chinese veto in the Security Council. On March 24, 1999, he announced that NATO was commencing air strikes against Serbia. The mission, as he defined it, was to deter a Serbian offensive against Kosovars "and, if necessary, to seriously damage the Serbian military's capacity to harm the people of Kosovo." Much to the relief of most Americans, as well as members of Congress, Clinton also flatly declared that he did not intend to put American troops in Kosovo to fight a war.

NATO's bombing campaign began as a well-intentioned effort to avoid a repeat of the murderous ethnic cleansing of Bosnia. Clinton and Albright hoped that several days of bombing would force Milosevic to bend to NATO's will, but he refused to yield to demands that he and most Serbs considered to be a gross violation of Yugoslavia's sovereign rights. Not having a viable alternative, then, NATO continued to bomb, in the hope that in time Serb forces in Kosovo would be sufficiently degraded and that damage to Serbia, including Belgrade itself, would be so costly that Milosevic would capitulate.

Unfortunately for the Albanian Kosovars, Clinton's decision led to the withdrawal of 1,300 observers monitoring Serb behavior on the ground in Kosovo. Their presence had more or less kept the situation under control. Worse yet, once the bombing began, Milosevic poured troops into Kosovo and allowed them to pursue a violent policy of ethnic cleansing. Although many thousands of Albanian Kosovars had fled Kosovo prior to the bombing campaign, NATO's air assault greatly exacerbated the situation by giving the Serbs a fresh opportunity to engage in a massive effort to drive the majority of Kosovars out of the province. By the time the war ended, an estimated 850,000 Kosovars had been expelled, creating a massive refugee problem throughout the region. At the same time, several thousand Kosovars had been killed by Milosevic's troops, as well as by NATO's bombing inside Kosovo.

Although NATO's bombing campaign failed to end hostilities quickly, it did achieve Clinton's separate goal of placating American public opinion, which was at best ambivalent about the war in Kosovo and strongly opposed to sending troops to do battle with the Serbs. Since Clinton had publicly rejected the use of ground troops, he relied solely on air power to achieve victory. The *New York Times* reported that "More than 33,000 missions took place; during 12,500 of them, bombs were dropped or missiles fired." No American pilot was lost or killed throughout the entire air campaign, which protected Clinton from any public outcry over casualties.

Such was the context for a furious domestic debate over the course of the war in a post–Cold War world. Odd groupings of ideologically and politically disparate individuals formed as a result of Clinton's intervention. On one side were those who endorsed the use of force in Kosovo, which included liberal writer Susan Sontag and William Kristol, the editor of the neoconservative *Weekly Standard*. Not only did they support Clinton's intervention in the name of human rights, but they favored a land war as well. On the other side were Tom Hayden, a 1960s-style radical, and Pat Buchanan, a spokesman for the Republican right. They denounced Clinton's intervention on the grounds that it was not in America's interest to fight such a war. And they strongly opposed the use of ground troops.

As the swirling debate about strategy and goals intensified at home, American-launched missiles hit the Chinese embassy in Belgrade in early May 1999, killing several embassy staffers. Manifesting understandable outrage, Beijing demanded an explanation as to how and why it happened. Washington answered by saying that the bombing was an unfortunate accident. To limit a controversy that had stirred up considerable anti-American feeling in China, the United States not only apologized to Beijing but paid a cash indemnity to the Chinese government as well.

NATO's bombing campaign also strained American relations with Moscow, a longtime ally of Serbia. Nevertheless, Moscow provided NATO with indispensable assistance toward ending the conflict by bridging the negotiating chasm between Belgrade and NATO. Viktor Chernomyrdin, Moscow's representative to Belgrade, along with Martti Ahtisaari, the president of Finland, informed Milosevic that NATO was prepared to escalate the conflict. Fearing a ground war that Clinton might yet launch, Milosevic capitulated in early June. But NATO's new diplomatic terms made it easier for him to yield. The occupation of Kosovo would take place under the aegis of the United Nations Security Council, not NATO; the proposed referendum to decide the question of Kosovo's independence would be canceled; Serbia would retain de jure rights in several areas inside the province and would not be subject to NATO occupation at home; and the KLA would be disarmed. If such flexible negotiating terms had been on the table much earlier, Albanian Kosovars might have been spared the bombing, the forced flight, and the extensive collateral damage to their homeland that Secretary Albright's ultimatum, along with the KLA insurgency and Serbian repression, had helped to precipitate. Serb civilians living in Belgrade and elsewhere would not have been subjected to the repeated bombing attacks NATO unleashed as a result of that diplomatic impasse.

Nevertheless, on June 10, 1999, President Clinton declared that "we have achieved a victory for a safer world, for our democratic values and for a stronger America." In his eyes the credibility of NATO had been preserved, and the "one million" people driven out of Kosovo would now have the opportunity to return home with the protection of troops operating under the mandate of the United Nations Security Council. He also declared that as long as Milosevic, branded a war criminal by the War Crimes Tribunal, remained in power, the United States would provide no assistance to Serbia for reconstruction. Clinton failed to mention that Kosovo had become, like Bosnia, a NATO protectorate and that troops would remain there for years to come to prevent a further outbreak of violence between the Albanian Kosovars and the Serbs.

Although Clinton was deeply involved in policy matters pertaining to Kosovo, he did not ignore his domestic agenda. In April 1999, he sought to vindicate his policy of welfare reform by announcing that the number of people receiving welfare had dropped to 7.6 million, which represented a 38 percent decrease since 1996. He ignored a darker reality: only 60 percent of those who left welfare found jobs, and many lacked the skills and training that would allow them to survive the first recession to come. Some had been removed from the rolls for punitive reasons. Others receiving welfare benefits now faced time limits of five years, after which all federally mandated assistance would end. Neither Clinton nor other sponsors of welfare reform spent much time discussing publicly what would happen to those individuals who were incapable of finding work for mental or physical reasons and would eventually face termination of their federal benefits.

Associated with the issue of welfare was the matter of poverty, which remained entrenched and pervasive. Despite the big boom of the late 1990s, one out of every five children in America still lived in poverty. In the summer of 1999, Clinton tried to focus national attention on the issue while visiting various depressed areas of the country on a four-day junket. The trip attracted very little media coverage, even though much of what he had to say about the terrible conditions some

Americans had to confront in their daily lives rang true. Most Americans had no interest in the issue of poverty and no desire to repeat Lyndon Johnson's war on poverty. Nor did Bill Clinton for that matter. Having staked his political career on avoiding a liberal tag, he had fashioned a politically amorphous "third-way" approach to public policy issues, which, along with a cautious centrism, defined his ideological makeup. On the other hand, he did not eschew government support for the working poor, and fought hard for the earned income tax credit, which was the government's most effective anti poverty program. As sociologist Christopher Jencks remarked, "To move toward a more work-oriented system will make it a lot easier to get things done for poor people over the next 30 years." It now appeared that Clinton was in a stronger political position to request more support for social programs because voters no longer believed that tax dollars were being wasted on "welfare queens."

Meanwhile, the economy continued to hum. By November 1999, more than twenty million new jobs had been generated, matching the number created during the Reagan years. At the same time, serious inflation was contained, and productivity growth, amounting to over 2 percent a year, continued to astound. Unemployment fell to 4.1 percent, the lowest figure since January 1970. Also encouraging was the historic drop in black unemployment to 7.7 percent, teenage unemployment to 14.1 percent, and Hispanic unemployment to 6.9 percent.

The great job machine had thus provided opportunities for millions to enter the labor market for the first time. Falling unemployment reinforced a trend toward lower crime rates within the inner cities. Thanks to the extent and depth of the boom, workers at the bottom of the wage scale saw a slight improvement in their wages, even if their remuneration was far below the median wage of more than $13 an hour for many of the jobs that became available during the economy's new surge.

Those new jobs, created in a tightening labor market, did not spark an inflationary rise in unit labor costs, contrary to conventional wisdom and past history. Wages remained fairly constant as a result of a vastly weakened American labor movement, as well as widespread hiring of both legal and illegal immigrants at wages generally well below the national average. In early 2000, data confirmed that workers making $26 an hour or less (constituting 90 percent of the workforce) obtained a smaller wage increase in 1999—after adjustment for a minuscule rise in inflation—than they had in 1998. Yet Alan Greenspan, Federal Reserve Board chairman, worried that a serious inflationary upturn might be triggered by wage pressures, so he raised interest rates six times beginning in June 1999, hoping that this step would slow the economy. It continued to grow at a rapid clip, and the stock market, despite a correction or two, did not suffer a significant drop.

While Greenspan applied pressure to the economy's brake via monetary policy, the Clinton administration announced in late June that the projected budget surplus would reach $99 billion in 1999, $142 billion in 2000, and $2,926 trillion in ten years. Such was the context for the continuing budget battle between Clinton and Congress, with each side having a different agenda for spending that surplus. Clinton's agenda included a $250 billion tax cut over ten years to spur retirement savings for low- and middle-income families, a deep reduction in the federal debt, and the buttressing of Social Security and Medicare. Congressional Republicans, as usual, opted for a big ten-year tax cut of $792 billion.

During the Clinton years, the two sides had often engaged in a protracted struggle over the shape of the budget. Although Clinton had accepted the need for a balanced budget, debt reduction, and more money for the military, which were largely Republican objectives, he still saw the federal government as a positive and necessary instrument to improve people's lives in a complex and diverse society. The GOP, conversely, wanted to reduce Washington's role and influence in order to put more responsibility for economic growth in the hands of the states, localities, and individuals, whenever and wherever possible. Ironically, the elimination of the deficit—a longtime Republican goal—had generated a budgetary surplus, which now made it possible for Clinton to expand government programs in a manner more consistent with his outlook in 1993.

As each side sought to gain an advantage in the budgetary poker game, the best cards remained in President Clinton's hands because of his veto power. Using it more than thirty times by mid-1999, he had thwarted various Republican initiatives while gaining some Republican concessions to finance his own domestic agenda. Unable to overcome his veto and unwilling to shut down the government for the third time, the GOP in November 1999 finally agreed to a budget deal that gave both sides something they wanted. Clinton forced the Republicans to remove riders in the budget bill that would have placed commercial interests ahead of the environment. In addition, he obtained funding for new teachers and the hiring of more police, along with a partial payment of the American debt owed to the United Nations. Republicans could rightly claim that the Social Security trust fund remained intact, since it had not been tapped to finance any other programs. They also took credit for obtaining more money for the military and providing additional dollars for education. Yet both sides funded their respective programs so that they again broke the spending caps, mandated by the Balanced Budget Act of 1997, and pushed more than $20 billion into the next fiscal year.

Although Clinton managed to get some of what he wanted in a $1.8 trillion budget, he failed to get congressional approval for a number of the large-scale items such as a patient's bill of rights and a reform of Medicare. He had hoped to burnish his legacy with such major legislative accomplishments, but the fallout from impeachment had so poisoned his relationship with Republicans on Capitol Hill that the forging of a bipartisan coalition to get action on anything other than trade policy was now virtually beyond reach. Hence, opportunities to pass legislation on health care, gun control, the minimum wage, and campaign finance reform were held hostage to the requirements of partisan politics.

In this period, the White House worked in tandem with congressional Democrats, whose ultimate goal was to raise issues such as a patient's bill of rights, prescription drugs for seniors, and more funding for public education, which they could then take to the electorate in 2000. Making it easier for the two sides to cooperate was that Clinton's third way had won over many converts in his own party on matters such as crime, welfare reform, fiscal policy, and debt reduction, which helped to ease tensions between them. Only on trade was there still a deep and continuing disagreement between the White House and many Democrats on Capitol Hill. Otherwise, as the 2000 election approached, the Democratic Party was now ideologically well situated within Clinton's centrist fold.

Although Clinton found a way to mend fences with many in his own party in the House, it was a different story in the Senate, which on October 13, 1999, voted 51 to 48 to reject a treaty banning all underground nuclear testing. With a two-thirds majority vote needed for ratification, it was a stunning foreign policy defeat, which Clinton decried as a "reckless and partisan" act. Worried that this "isolationist" vote, engineered by the Republican leadership, would have countries "abandoning the nonproliferation treaty," he declared that the United States would continue to abide by a moratorium on testing and would seek a permanent ban on all such testing. Speaking after the Senate had voted, Republican Majority Leader Trent Lott called the treaty "dangerous." He and his fellow Republicans believed that it would not prevent "rogue states" like North Korea from testing its weapons at a time when the United States was bound by treaty obligations not to do the same.

That vote reflected the deep undercurrent of hostility between Republicans and Clinton as a result of his impeachment, but both the Clinton White House and most Republicans still shared the common goal of reaching a trade accommodation with China. In mid-November, the administration finally settled its various differences with China, which opened both sides to a wider exchange of goods and investment opportunities. But the agreement had to be approved by Congress, which would have to forgo its annual review of China's trade status.

Remembering the fight over ratification of NAFTA, the White House and the Business Roundtable began to mobilize their resources to pressure recalcitrant members of the House—mostly Democrats—to vote for the treaty. In the meantime, eyes were focused on Seattle, where the World Trade Organization (WTO) was to hold its meeting in early December to address a variety of international trade issues. Although President Clinton had earlier promised Chinese President Jiang Zemin that he would push for Chinese admission to the WTO, other developments quickly took center stage. Strong opposition from organized labor and environmental activists to the WTO and its secret administration of world trade rules and regulations sparked major demonstrations and marches on the streets of Seattle and quickly captured headlines around the globe. As a result of this new environmental and labor coalition, a dynamic social movement appeared to have taken root, one that Bill Clinton could no longer safely ignore. As Jeffrey Garten, a former Clinton administration official, observed, "This movement's power and influence are going to grow steadily . . . globalization has become a major issue that no longer interests only pundits and academics. It's entered the mainstream of popular concern."

Using economic power for strategic ends in a manner that went beyond all of his predecessors, Clinton had hoped to come away from

Seattle with an agreement that would define the shape and terms of world trade into the next century. As the demonstrations unfolded, however, he acknowledged the need to incorporate labor and environmental concerns into future trade agreements reached by the WTO. Clinton obviously worried about maintaining support from key interest groups, such as the AFL-CIO and the Sierra Club, which were central to Democratic political fortunes in 2000.

Despite Clinton's hopes, the Seattle meeting went badly, as many undeveloped nations railed against environmental and labor standards they found impossible to meet. Also, major industrial powers were at loggerheads on a variety of trade issues. Thus, with no consensus in sight and with the WTO under serious assault, the White House accepted defeat because it feared alienating the AFL-CIO by making a deal that failed to include a study group within the WTO to examine workers' rights. Unlike its struggle against NAFTA, the AFL-CIO had Clinton on its side in this fight, largely as a result of his desire to placate labor on the eve of the primary season. He was mindful of the organization's earlier endorsement of Vice President Al Gore for the Democratic presidential nomination and did not want to complicate Gore's relationship with labor or environmental groups.

Labor, a key bloc inside the national Democratic Party, had made something of a comeback, thanks to the inspired leadership of John Sweeney, the president of the AFL-CIO. He pushed hard to recruit new members at a time when only 13.9 percent of the total workforce belonged to unions. Furthermore, he began to focus labor's attention on issues and concerns that had a broader national appeal, such as increasing the minimum wage and reversing the continuing stagnation of wages for a majority of working Americans. During his tenure, Sweeney also functioned as a linchpin for formerly antagonistic groups, such as unions and environmental organizations. As a result of sharing a common hostility to the rule-making authority of the WTO, their interests began to converge at the same time that larger numbers of Americans, facing downsizing and wage stagnation, now viewed organized labor more sympathetically than at any time since the Reagan era. Whether this mood would translate into major recruitment gains for organized labor was still too soon to say. Nevertheless, Democrats still needed labor's money and organizational skill if they were to do well in any closely contested national election.

While Clinton worked hard to keep labor on board, despite sharp differences between them over his trade bill with China, he also reached out to win the support of environmental groups. He forced Republicans to drop a number of antienvironmental riders from their 1999 budget, and he used his authority under the National Antiquities Act of 1906 to create new national monuments in the West and to protect land from those who would plunder precious federal holdings solely for private gain. By the time he was through, Clinton had placed more land in the lower forty-eight states under federal protection as national monuments than any other president in the twentieth century, including Theodore Roosevelt. With this action, he laid down a marker for future presidents to follow.

The case with civil rights was similar. Clinton advanced that cause with evident conviction, building on the warm and friendly relationships he had with African Americans. During his presidency he appointed several black Americans to key positions in his administration, and he protected affirmative action as a means of advancing minority employment. Understandably, black Americans strongly supported Clinton throughout his impeachment ordeal, given his positive record on racial issues. As Harvard Professor Henry Louis Gates remarked, "we are going to the wall with this President." Blacks understood that Bill Clinton had ultimately protected them from the worst of the Gingrich revolution, and they recognized that black unemployment during the Clinton years had been reduced to levels not seen in several decades.

Despite Clinton's salutary efforts on behalf of African Americans, there remained a side to their story that attracted little national attention or interest, much less comprehension. Even during the good times of the late 1990s, income and wealth levels among black, Hispanic, and white Americans remained vastly disparate. In fact, although the income gap had closed slightly between black and white families by the late 1990s, the *New York Times* reported in 1998 that "The typical white family earned about $47,000 in 1996, almost twice that of blacks. Worse, the typical black household had a net worth of only about $4,500, a tenth of the white figure." Furthermore, in a period of the greatest run-up in stock prices in market history, which benefited many white households, about 95 percent of black families owned no stock or pension funds. Clinton was, of course, unable to do anything about a form of racial inequality that was determined far more by class relations and property ownership than by the labor market. But he supported an increase in the minimum wage and the enhancement of the earned income tax credit, which had already helped poor working black and white families improve their precarious financial situation.

President Clinton also prepared an agenda for his final year in office in a determined effort to overcome the stigma of impeachment. As that work proceeded, his positive job rating stood at 63 percent, even though 64 percent did not approve of him personally. The polls also pointed to the moderate political consensus at work in American politics that Clinton had done much to shape. Fifty percent of the public favored the continuation of his centrist policies, 33 percent wanted a more conservative approach, but only 10 percent desired a more liberal government. Such, then, was the broad political context for Clinton's final State of the Union address, which he delivered to Congress on January 27, 2000.

Appearing in the House chamber where he had been impeached thirteen months earlier, Clinton, with posterity in mind, declared that

> We restored the vital center, replacing outdated ideologies with a new vision anchored in basic enduring values: opportunity for all, responsibility from all and a community of all Americans. . . . We begin the new century with over 20 million new jobs. The fastest economic growth in more than 30 years; the lowest unemployment rates in 30 years; the lowest poverty rates in 20 years; the lowest African-American and Hispanic unemployment rates on record; the first back to back budget surpluses in 42 years. Next month, America will achieve the longest period of economic growth in our entire history. We have built a new economy.

After noting those accomplishments, Clinton called on Congress to fund prescription drug coverage to all Medicare recipients, to increase the minimum wage, and to pass a patient's bill of rights. Here, then, was the agenda Clinton pushed in order to make himself relevant in a political year that would otherwise be dominated by his promotion of Vice President Al Gore's bid for the presidency.

As usual, Clinton's performance was masterful on the tactical level. He co-opted the Republican call for a tax cut with one of his own, and he joined Republicans by supporting the easing of the marriage penalty, which would allow married couples to file tax returns jointly without paying more in taxes than did separate single filers. On the largely Republican issue of debt reduction, he remained true to form by once again announcing that he would spend the huge surpluses projected for the coming years to pay down the federal debt.

Clinton's speech was attacked by Texas Governor George Bush, the front-runner for the Republican presidential nomination, as a "litany for spending." How much to be spent was spelled out in detail when Clinton submitted his eighth budget to Congress on February 7, 2000. Proposing nearly $1.9 trillion on a variety of programs, Clinton nevertheless contended that his was "a balanced budget with a balanced approach to our national problems. It maintains our fiscal discipline, pays down the debt, extends the life of Social Security and Medicare, and invests in our families and our future." Specifically, Clinton proposed $291 billion for the Defense Department and $875 billion for the various entitlement programs, including Social Security and Medicare. Nonmilitary discretionary spending would receive $355 billion, and interest on the national debt $208 billion. And from a projected surplus of $184 billion, $160 billion—coming from Social Security—would be used for debt reduction.

Not surprisingly, Republicans were extremely critical of Clinton's budget, decrying it as another "tax and spend" big government document. Governor Bush remarked that Clinton's proposals made his point "that surpluses will be spent if we don't have a leader who's willing to cut taxes." And Republican House Speaker J. Dennis Hastert asked: "How can we pay down the debt with a budget that substantially expands the size and scope of the federal government? . . . How can the era of big government be over when his budget would create close to $350 billion in new government programs?"

Hastert's questions were on the mark. Clinton's budget supported many domestic programs, especially health care, and pointed to an enhanced role for government. Having learned his lesson from the bitter defeat of his health plan in 1994, he was prepared to move step-by-step on all fronts and he was gaining ground. Stuart Butler of the conservative Heritage Foundation observed that Clinton's incremental approach had persuaded Congress to accept changes in domestic policy. Said Butler: "I wouldn't say it's more palatable but it's harder to resist. It's directed at very tangible aspects of people's lives. The president can say he's just solving people's problems, not expanding the role of government." Thomas E. Mann of the Brookings Institution also saw something similar at work. "It is amazing what Clinton has achieved. He really has repositioned the party, and he's used fiscal conservatism as a tool of activist government. Activist government, however, is re-defined in more modest terms."

Although Clinton's budget dismayed virtually all Republicans, some Democrats, including former Secretary of Labor Robert Reich, were upset with his focus on debt reduction at the expense of adding even more funds to Head Start programs, education, and health care. Reich believed that the magnitude of the problems facing the country, and the prospect of huge budget surpluses for years to come, should have prompted Clinton to invest greater sums in the public sector. Clinton's approach, Reich thought, "is bad economics, and it's staggeringly bad policy when the country is so wealthy. To make debt elimination a new goal is to put a straitjacket on any future public ambitions." Reich saw Clinton's policies as reminiscent of Calvin Coolidge, the fiscally arch-conservative Republican president of the 1920s.

Clinton responded to the criticism he received from left and right. "Some have said I sound like Calvin Coolidge, and others say that I am using it as an excuse to spend money on Americans. All I know is it works. If we get this country out of debt, it means the American people can borrow money at lower interest rates to invest in new businesses, to pay their home loans, to pay their car loans." He also reminded critics such as Reich that his budget included significant investments on behalf of children, the poor, and the elderly. But he never discussed what might happen to the economy if fiscal policy were driven by debt reduction in a period of recession.

In the meantime, Vice President Al Gore, under attack in the Democratic primaries by former Senator Bill Bradley, remarked that he would opt for debt reduction even in the face of a recession. Gore also insisted that Bradley's support of expansionist social programs, particularly in the area of health care, was not fiscally sound and ran the risk of damaging Medicaid coverage for poor citizens by undermining the program's integrity. Bradley, outspoken on the issue, shared Reich's concern that in an age of fiscal surpluses, the government should do much more than just tinker at the edges of social policy. He furthermore strongly supported campaign finance reform, suggesting that if he were the nominee he would not have to bear the burden of being identified with an administration involved with the large-scale campaign corruption of 1996.

Despite Bradley's best effort, he could not persuade a majority of Democrats that he deserved their vote. Gore, supported by organized labor and strongly assisted by the White House, won the Iowa caucuses as well as a narrow victory in the New Hampshire primary. From that point on, Bradley's effort to capture the nomination faltered. His campaign appeared increasingly to lack focus, energy, and appeal. On Super Tuesday—March 7, 2000—Gore won a sufficient number of delegates from California, New York, and elsewhere to lay claim to the nomination of his party. Having walked out of Bill Clinton's shadow, Gore now hoped to advance their shared centrist agenda with a victory in November.

Texas Governor George W. Bush was the early favorite to win the Republican nomination. While championing the cause of "compassionate conservatism," he had accumulated a vast sum from private sources to finance his campaign. In addition, he was backed by the Republican establishment, which saw him as the party's best hope of defeating Gore. Although Bush began his campaign with those distinct advantages, he soon discovered that his quest for the nomination was not akin to a coronation. As it turned out, the GOP contest produced bitter recriminations and hard-fought battles.

The strongest of the candidates challenging Bush was Arizona Senator John McCain, who appeared to many as a war hero because of his five years spent in a Hanoi prison. In addition, McCain was a good campaigner and an articulate proponent of campaign finance reform. Although his views were generally in accord with conservative Republican positions on abortion, gun control, and lower taxes, he was no hero to many of his fellow Republicans on Capitol Hill. His maverick style and tough talk on campaign finance reform had antagonized many of them. At the same time, McCain's public persona attracted a considerable following among many independent voters and some Democrats in New Hampshire, who were unhappy with the current state of American politics, and who were willing to embrace a candidate promising change and reform. McCain scored a stunning 19-point victory over Bush in the New Hampshire Republican primary, winning some votes that might otherwise have gone to Bradley.

Bush bounced back in South Carolina, where, in a very conservative Republican state, he triumphed decisively over McCain. But even though he later lost the Michigan primary to McCain, who again benefited from Democratic crossover votes, Bush soon moved ahead virtually everywhere else. He locked up his party's nomination with big victories on Super Tuesday, thanks to the strong support he received from

Republican voters in primaries where crossover voting was not permitted. Subsequently, Bush sought to mollify McCain and finally won a grudging endorsement in May. At the same time, he pulled slightly ahead of Gore in the polls because voters saw him projecting a greater capacity for leadership than the vice president.

While the primary season was under way, Clinton did what he could to aid Gore. He spoke out about the extraordinary growth of the American economy and attributed to Gore strong support for deficit reduction, which helped to make that boom possible. And he framed discussions bearing on gun control and taxes in such a way as to benefit Gore at the expense of Bush. Clinton was also focused on a major, if not historic, debate in Congress as to whether to grant China normal access to American markets without forcing it to undergo a yearly review by Congress on such matters as human rights.

An ad hoc coalition of liberal Democrats and conservative Republicans in the House complicated passage of the China bill. Liberal Democrats, strongly backed by organized labor, feared a flood of cheap goods into the American market from China. They were also highly critical of China's human rights record. Conservative Republicans, alarmed by China's belligerent rhetoric directed against Taiwan, wanted to retain leverage over China via the annual review of its trade status with the United States. And like many opposing Democrats, such as Minority Leader Richard Gephardt, they also condemned China's human rights record.

Unfortunately for the Democrats, that debate threatened their unity in an election year. Worried about the potential for job losses at home and the lack of human rights in China, they agreed that the bill was an "outright attempt to protect profits without any concern for human rights and workers' rights." On that issue, Gore was caught in the middle. Although Gore had already won labor's backing, which helped him defeat Bill Bradley in the primaries, he shared Clinton's views about the need to pass the measure in order to better political and commercial relations with China. So he gave it his endorsement, albeit in a quiet manner.

On May 24, 2000, the House voted 237 to 197 to approve normal trade rights with China. But only 73 of the 237 votes came from Democrats, far fewer than had been the case when NAFTA won House passage in November 1993. Thus, thanks to the support given the bill by a huge bloc of Republicans, Clinton achieved a major victory, consistent with his tactic of using trade to promote political and economic ends. In this case, Clinton argued that by normalizing trade relations with China and admitting it to the WTO, the power and rule of the Communist Party in China would be substantially weakened in the long run by market-driven priorities and goals. Committed to the politics of strategic engagement, he claimed that "We will have more positive influence with an outstretched hand than with a clenched fist." He also believed that "when over 100 million people in China can get on the Net, it will be impossible to maintain a closed political and economic society."

Yet, apart from Clinton's rhetoric and logrolling, and intense pressure from the business community, the bill passed the House because many saw it generating fresh opportunities for "American energy, gas, construction, telecommunications, and engineering firms" to do business in China. This legislation, they believed, would promote jobs in their respective congressional districts.

With the bill normalizing trade relations with China assured of easy passage in the Senate, Clinton moved to the next major item on his agenda. A highly controversial matter, it required him to decide whether the United States would employ a limited nuclear defense system to protect the country from a possible nuclear missile attack from a "rogue state" such as North Korea or Iraq. If he agreed to construct such a system, it would violate the Anti-Ballistic Missile Treaty, which Richard Nixon had successfully negotiated with the Soviet Union in 1972 and which prohibited the sort of antimissile program now under consideration at the White House. When Clinton traveled to Moscow in June 2000 to discuss the matter with Vladimir Putin, the new president of Russia, he found that Putin was strongly opposed to amending the ABM treaty, saying that the "cure" was worse than the disease.

Putin had a point. Moreover, public figures in NATO countries agreed with Putin's argument that any American move that threatened the treaty was unwise, as it could destabilize the nuclear environment by promoting a nuclear arms buildup in both Russia and China. At the same time, the prospect of constructing a workable defense against a rogue attack, in skies flooded with decoys, seemed fanciful at best, and it was all too reminiscent of Ronald Reagan's argument for undertaking the Strategic Defense Initiative, which few scientists ever thought was technically feasible.

Although the Defense Department had little or no success in constructing an operational missile defense system during either the Reagan years the Clinton presidency, domestic politics had driven the issue to the forefront once more. Clinton had increased Pentagon spending in 1999 by $10.5 billion over a six-year period for a limited national missile defense (NMD) program, fearing a Republican charge that his administration was soft on defense. In the meantime, Al Gore had moved out in front of Clinton and endorsed the construction of a limited system, costing possibly $60 billion. However, George W. Bush outdid him, having an even more grandiose scheme in mind. As he put it, "Our missile defense must be designated to protect all 50 states and our friends and allies and deployed forces overseas from missile attacks by rogue nations and accidental launches." Journalist David Corn noted that "if the limited system being explored by Clinton might cost up to $60 billion, the Bush plan, which would have to cover Japan, South Korea, Taiwan, Europe, and Israel, will cost several times that."

Backed by members of the Republican establishment, including Henry Kissinger and George Shultz, former secretaries of state, Bush communicated his views on NMD to the public, which generally supported the building of a missile defense system. At the same time, speaking on behalf of a "compassionate conservatism," he strengthened his position with many voters by avoiding the strident language and harsh tones associated with Newt Gingrich. While advocating the need to protect Medicare and provide prescription drugs for the elderly, he fully embraced mainstream Republican positions on tax cuts, national missile defense, and Social Security. Consequently, the *National Review*, an organ of Republican conservatism, declared that Bush was the right choice because he "has been reliably conservative on the issues that matter." It opined, for example, that Bush's "support for tax cuts and Social Security reform is more important than his spending initiatives—not the least because if he succeeds on taxes and Social Security, it will be easier to limit government in the future."

While Bush consolidated his lead in the polls, in moves reminiscent of Clinton's adroit maneuvering in 1992, Gore sought to unite Democrats under his banner. But he faced the challenge that many liberal Democrats did not like or trust him. Nor were they particularly fond of the Clinton administration's centrist social and economic policies, which Gore had fully supported. Seeking to address their concerns, he spoke out about the need to challenge and confront the "powerful interests lined up against us—from the big oil companies to the HMOs to the polluters." Whether this populist theme would attract voters was difficult to determine. Clinton had deliberately avoided such a stark appeal in 1996, fearing that it was too divisive and would quickly alienate voters.

Of concern to Gore was the support that disaffected Democrats were giving to Ralph Nader, the longtime champion of public interest regulation and staunch opponent of corporate hegemony, who was the nominee of the Green Party. Gore and his supporters feared that Nader, supported by 7 percent nationally in the polls, could cost him the election in a tight race. Dismissing Gore's concern, Nader stated that there were "very few major differences" between the nominees of the two major parties. He contended that "The corporate power structure dominates both parties and determines the limits of their meager initiatives." He argued that "The Clinton–Gore record offers no real hope for changing the concentration of power by the few over the needs of the many."

While Nader's candidacy posed a threat to Gore, Bill Clinton was doing his best to stay relevant and busy while seeking to help his vice president. He knew that a Gore victory would be viewed as part of his legacy, as much as Ronald Reagan understood that a George Bush victory in 1988 was also an endorsement by the voters of his own administration. Clinton's affair with Monica Lewinsky was a not-so-hidden issue in the election, as many Americans, wanting a higher moral tone in the White House, responded to Bush's call for fresh leadership in the Oval Office. Yet voters still gave the president a high job approval rating, thanks to a very good economy.

Statistics told the story. The economy grew at a remarkable 5.6 percent in the second quarter of 2000, unemployment remained steady at 4.1 percent, inflation was not a serious threat, corporate profits were impressive, and stock prices, despite fluctuations, still stood at near-record high levels. There were some disquieting developments, however. Yale University economist Robert Shiller pointed out that stock prices were far higher than current corporate profits and dividends warranted or justified. Concurrently, corporate debt in 2000 stood at $10.6 trillion, while consumer debt reached $7.5 trillion, with at least a quarter of all new mortgages going to people who are "basically broke," remarked one informed observer. The extraordinary jump in the merchandise trade deficit (exports minus imports) reached a record $30.6 billion in June 2000, while the current account deficit, which includes foreign trade and goods and services, was running at an annual rate of approximately $435 billion. Because of America's insatiable appetite for borrowing abroad, money owed to foreign investors had climbed to over 20 percent of the gross domestic product, amounting to a historic high of $1.6 trillion.

Those worrisome trends notwithstanding, the Republicans were full of optimism at their convention in Philadelphia, where they warmly embraced Governor Bush's selection of Dick Cheney as his vice presidential running mate. A former secretary of defense in President George H. W. Bush's Cabinet during the period of the Gulf War, Cheney had also served six terms in the House. There, he voted against a nonbinding resolution calling for the freeing of Nelson Mandela from a South African prison, opposed funding for Head Start, and consistently supported pro-life proposals. Cheney's voting record was less important to Bush than the fact that he was knowledgeable about how to do business in Washington, that he was a loyal and unobtrusive team player, and that Bush's father, the former president, wanted him on the ticket.

That Bush had learned well from Clinton was evident both in the tone of the Republican Convention and in his acceptance speech. Moving toward a new Republican center, the convention managers sharply rejected the harsh right-wing rhetoric of 1996. At the same time, Bush's well-crafted and well-delivered address was geared to broadening the support for the party by stressing the need for "inclusiveness" and compassionate conservatism. Thus, he intended "to put conservative values and conservative ideas into the thick of the fight for justice and opportunity." At the same time, his agenda included the promise of upright behavior in the Oval Office, a ten-year tax cut of $1.3 trillion, the partial privatizing of Social Security, and the use of vouchers to confront the serious problems affecting public education in America.

Following the Republican Convention, Gore had fallen well behind Bush in the polls and needed a big boost to get back in the race. Drawing favorable attention to his campaign was his announcement on August 8 that Senator Joseph Lieberman of Connecticut would be his running mate. The current chairman of the Democratic Leadership Council, Lieberman was the first Jewish American ever included on a national ticket by either major political party. Although Lieberman's voting record was generally more conservative than that of most northern Democrats in the Senate, Gore picked him because he had delivered a speech to the Senate, on September 3, 1998, denouncing Clinton's behavior in the Lewinsky affair. With this adroit move, Gore appeared to head off Republican attacks directed at Clinton's behavior and his own close association with the president.

In his acceptance speech, Gore also sought to separate himself from Clinton, declaring that he was running for the presidency as his "own man." Outlining his agenda, which included the need to protect Social Security, Medicare, and *Roe v. Wade*, he warned that reckless tax cuts could endanger the surplus and damage the prosperity that Americans had experienced during the Clinton years. Along with his selection of Lieberman, he made up ground with that acceptance speech in which he declared that "They are for the powerful. We are for the people." With his lagging campaign for the presidency now revived, he pulled ahead of Bush in the polls.

While the two presidential nominees prepared for the fall campaign and the debates to come, Clinton announced on September 1 that he was postponing action to construct a national missile shield and would leave the matter in the hands of the next president. In making his decision, he stated that although the threat of future missile attacks from states like North Korea and Iraq "is real and growing," the United States "should not move forward until we have absolute confidence the system will work." Many NATO allies of the United States welcomed this move because they feared that the construction of such a system could precipitate a dangerous new arms race with both Russia and China in offensive nuclear weapons.

Although Clinton was busy with foreign affairs, he did not ignore domestic matters: he vetoed Republican-sponsored marriage tax and estate tax legislation because, in his view, wealthier Americans, rather than those from farther down the income scale, were the major beneficiaries of these tax cuts. In addition, he asserted that the loss of money to the federal government as a result of those tax cuts would make it more difficult to fund programs such as Medicare and education. The House's failure to override his vetoes by the necessary two-thirds vote once again underscored the importance of the veto as a weapon in the presidential arsenal during a period of divided government and intense partisanship.

While Clinton was battling with Congress, the Office of Independent Counsel, after completing a nearly $60 million investigation, made public its Whitewater report. On September 20, Robert Ray, Kenneth Starr's successor, announced that there was "insufficient" evidence to conclude that the Clintons had engaged in wrongdoing or illegal behavior in the Whitewater case. Since he could not prove their guilt in a jury trial beyond a reasonable doubt, he had no plans to take legal action against them. Ray's carefully worded statement came at the right time for Hillary Clinton, because it removed at once a potentially serious impediment to her recently launched campaign to win an open Senate seat from New York resulting from the retirement of Senator Daniel Patrick Moynihan.

President Clinton also received more good news during the first week of October. The Serbian people, in a nonviolent uprising, forced Slobodan Milosevic to step down as president of Serbia after he refused to accept the results of a first-ballot victory won by his opponent, Vojislav Kostunica, in a freely contested election. Although Kostunica himself was a staunch Serb nationalist who opposed the NATO bombing of Serbia and supported Serb control of Kosovo, he was a strong defender of the rule of law. His triumph, which stood as a decisive victory for opposition forces in Serbia, cleared the way for Yugoslavia to ultimately reestablish viable political and economic connections with the rest of Europe and the United States.

With Clinton minding White House business, the presidential campaign picked up steam as each side hoped to gain an advantage from the three presidential debates. As a result of his performance in those debates, Bush pulled slightly ahead of Gore in the polls. Much to the surprise of observers, he appeared not just likable but well enough informed to quell the doubts of many voters who wondered whether he had the right stuff to handle the responsibilities and pressures that went with the presidency. He was also helped by his approach to public policy issues, such as Social Security, education, and drug benefits for seniors, which managed to allay the fears of many voters that he was just another hard-line conservative. By pushing a Republican version of Clintonism, not Newt Gingrich's harsher and more ideologically driven agenda from the right, Bush gave the appearance that he was really more of a centrist and a moderate at heart. At the same time, he said his goal was to bring dignity back to the office of the presidency and to provide fresh leadership in Washington so as to overcome the partisan bickering and deadlock that currently prevailed in Congress.

Al Gore lost traction during the debates. Not only did his debating style grate on people, they did not respond well to his verbal exaggerations, which tended to benefit Bush. Worse, while most voters were satisfied with the current state of the economy, Gore did not politically profit from the boom that had occurred after 1995, because a majority of Americans thought that the private sector, not the Clinton–Gore administration, was largely responsible for the good times currently prevailing. Yet he sought to emphasize during the debates that the dynamic economy would be imperiled if Bush became president. He also spoke out against Bush's tax cut, which mostly benefited the richest Americans. He opposed the use of vouchers for parents seeking to find alternatives to often failing public education systems. And he endorsed a drug program for seniors that appeared to provide more benefits than Bush's. In addition, he took a strong pro-choice stand on abortion and defended measures to protect the environment. At the heart of his agenda for the future was a strong commitment to reducing national debt within a decade or so.

Notwithstanding the fact that there were real, albeit narrow, differences in policy separating these two candidates, voters in general were discontented and bored with both of them. So even though the parties and their supporters spent $3 billion on this election, only 51 percent of eligible voters turned out at the polls. Those voters, reflecting the deep political, cultural, and regional divisions at work in the country, produced one of the most closely contested elections in American history, with Al Gore and George W. Bush effectively ending up in a tie.

Although Gore ultimately commanded a 539,000-vote in the nationwide popular vote, Bush held on to a narrow lead of less than a thousand votes in Florida, which became the pivotal state in the 2000 presidential election. If Bush were to win Florida, it would give him the state's 25 electoral votes and a victory in the Electoral College, with a one-vote margin over the required minimum of 270. Whereas if Al Gore won Florida, having already put 267 electoral votes in his pocket, he would be Bill Clinton's successor in the White House.

As a recount of ballots began, Gore was in trouble because there were many ballots ostensibly cast for him that could not be included in any final total as a result of either ballot irregularities or confusion on the part of voters using an oddly designed ballot in largely Democratic Palm Beach County. There, several thousand voters intending to vote for Gore mistakenly ended up voting for Pat Buchanan, the Reform Party candidate, because they misread a ballot that had been approved earlier by a Democratic Party official.

Facing certain defeat, Gore sought relief in the Florida Supreme Court, asking it to set aside an earlier certification of the Florida vote for Bush by the Florida secretary of state, until hand counts of votes had been completed in several largely Democratic counties, including Broward and Palm Beach. He contended, not improperly, that machines using punch card ballots did not always accurately register voter intention, which might best be revealed by a hand count. The court granted him a few extra days to proceed with the hand count in those counties until it was time to certify the finality of the election results, but it later blocked his efforts to continue with a hand recount in mostly Democratic Miami-Dade County.

President Clinton encouraged Gore to continue with his legal challenges, but Republicans were furious with Democratic tactics, claiming that Gore was seeking to "steal" the election by hand counts. In their view, hand counting lacked standard or uniform criteria for rendering an objective judgment. Thus, if Gore were to win Florida by this method, Bob Dole said that Republicans might "boycott" his inaugural. With the situation becoming increasingly acrimonious and ugly, and with both sides showing little restraint in their continuing legal battle, there was still no declared winner in the presidential race even after the Thanksgiving holiday.

Then, in a historically unprecedented move, the U.S. Supreme Court entered Florida's election thicket. The Court granted a review to George W. Bush's petition asking it to overturn the Florida Supreme Court decision allowing hand-counted ballots to be added to Florida's total vote count even though that vote had already been certified by Florida's secretary of state. On December 4, it overruled the action of the Florida Supreme Court and asked that court to clarify the reasoning behind its earlier decision. Concurrently, decisions taken by other Florida courts derailed Gore's hopes of gaining a recount based on hand-counted ballots. Although the Florida Supreme Court intervened to allow a hand count of ballots to proceed in several counties, the U.S. Supreme Court, driven by its conservative wing, stayed that count while it prepared to hear lawyers for Bush and Gore argue the case for and against the merits of the recount process. In rendering its decision, the highest federal court remanded the case back to Florida's Supreme Court, declaring that that court had failed to adhere to the equal protection clause of the Constitution in allowing recounts to proceed without a uniform standard of judgment. But with time running out before Florida's 25 electoral votes were to be legislatively delivered to Bush, the U.S. Supreme Court, in a 5-to-4 decision, then effectively slammed the door on Gore's chances of winning the state. Having now lost Florida by 537 votes, Gore conceded the election to Governor Bush.

Although Democrats were disheartened by the loss of the presidency, they managed to win four new Senate seats to tie the GOP, 50–50, in the Senate. They fell short of capturing the House, thereby leaving the Republicans—as before—with a very narrow majority in that chamber. Even though the GOP now controlled both the White House and Congress for the first time since the election of 1952, it seemed unlikely that the prevailing deadlock in Congress would be easily broken any time soon.

Bill Clinton, thinking of his legacy, wanted Gore to win, and he tried to help him. Gore had limited Clinton's campaign activities, probably because he was afraid that Clinton would resurrect the character issue in a way 'that Bush could use to his benefit. Thus, operating on a short leash, Clinton appeared in just a few localities in an attempt to mobilize support for Gore. Whether he might have changed the outcome of the election if he had campaigned actively in his home state of Arkansas and elsewhere is difficult to determine. Like Gore's Tennessee, Clinton's Arkansas was another one of the many southern states carried by Bush in the election.

Although Gore's defeat was bad news for Clinton, Hillary Clinton's victory in the race for a Senate seat from New York was good news. It marked the first time in American history that a first lady had won an election. Thanks to her success, she now embarked on a political career in national politics, which would keep her constantly in the limelight as a possible future candidate for the Democratic presidential nomination. As Bill Clinton's political career was ending, hers was beginning.

While the legal storm over Florida's recount grew in intensity, Clinton visited Vietnam in mid-November. His efforts at reconciliation looked to the betterment of relations between the two countries, which he had set in motion earlier in his presidency. He avoided discussing the past and refused to apologize for American actions during the Vietnam War. While speaking in Hanoi he urged Vietnam to integrate as fast as possible into the world economy and thus, presumably, become a consumer of American goods and a recipient of American investment capital.

During the final weeks of his presidency, Clinton and Congress completed work on the last stages of the 2001 budget. The fiscal surplus made it easier to forge that agreement and allowed both sides to add money to programs they wanted. Clinton, for example, obtained increased spending for such key programs as Head Start, school construction, and the hiring of new teachers. In addition, Medicare received a substantial increase, and children from low-income families would now find it easier to obtain health benefits through Medicaid and the Children's Health Insurance Program. And the legal status of nearly 700,000 immigrants was temporarily restored thanks to this legislation.

Clinton extracted concessions from a Republican Congress fearful of precipitating another government shutdown. The agreement was not quite as good from his perspective as an earlier deal that fell through, but he still praised the results: "It is a budget that is fiscally responsible, pays down the debt and makes vital investments in our nation's future. In education, health care, and community renewal, this budget provides more opportunity for more Americans than ever before."

Although the gains Clinton celebrated were not nearly as far-reaching as he wanted, they did represent progress. An incrementalist at heart, he believed that "If you are willing to win in inches as well as feet, a phenomenal amount of positive things can happen." Such had largely been Clinton's approach to policy making ever since the disaster of health care in 1994 and the Gingrich revolution that followed. In short, his modus operandi had both protected and strengthened several programs at the heart of the welfare state, however small scale and limited those improvements were in actual practice.

As Clinton prepared to leave office, it appeared that the bloom was beginning to fade from the economic rose. Economic growth for the third quarter of 2000 averaged only 2.2 percent, which was down considerably from the 5.6 percent of the second quarter. At the same time, job layoffs in such important companies as General Motors were on the rise even though unemployment still remained at

4 percent. Still, Clinton's job approval rating stood at a remarkable 65 percent in January 2001, largely as a result of the greatest economic boom in American history.

Even with such a rating, Clinton still faced the threat of a post-presidential prosecution resulting from his testimony about Monica Lewinsky in the Paula Jones sexual harassment lawsuit. Making a deal with Robert Ray, the independent counsel, to avoid any such prosecution, Clinton, on his last full day in office, publicly declared that his responses "to questions about Ms. Lewinsky were false." In order to end the possibility of disbarment in his home state, he also agreed to a five-year suspension of his Arkansas law license and the payment of a $25,000 fine to cover counsel fees.

Ray welcomed Clinton's statement because he "has admitted that he knowingly gave evasive and misleading answers . . . and has acknowledged that some of his answers were false." Believing that the nation's interests had been served by Clinton's action, Ray closed his office, declaring that "This matter is now concluded. May history and the American people judge that it has been concluded justly."

On January 20, 2001, Bill Clinton became the youngest ex-president since Theodore Roosevelt. Americans looking back on his years as president would surely remember his impeachment. Nor would they forget some of his last-minute pardons, such as that of Marc Rich, a billionaire fugitive living in Switzerland, who broke embargoes to trade with Iran and Libya. In Clinton's favor, however, was the reality that he had served his country generally as a peacemaker, whose efforts coincided, for the first time since the 1960s, with a full-employment economy. Could or would any of his successors leave such an enviable record as part of their legacy?

Conclusion

The story of the Clinton presidency is replete with irony and para-dox. Coming to power in January 1993, Bill Clinton sought to over-come the conservative legacy of Ronald Reagan. Instead, he helped to consolidate the Reagan revolution by reforming welfare and bal-ancing the budget. While Clinton's failed health care program and support of gays in the military gave the Republicans an opportunity to win back Congress in 1994, their own overreaching provided him with the opening he needed to win reelection in 1996. Following Clinton's impeachment, a majority of voters expressed their personal disapproval of him, yet they continued to give him a high job ap-proval rating as a result of the good economy.

The matter of Clinton's impeachment is, of course, a key issue over which historians and policy analysts began to argue even before Clin-ton left office. Historian Stanley Kutler contends, for example, that, in the face of the considerable Republican effort to drive Clinton from of-fice, Clinton's lasting contribution to the preservation of the American constitutional order was his categorical refusal to resign at a time when there was already serious talk in some quarters that such a step might become necessary. Still, Clinton's impeachment continued the long-term loss of presidential prestige that began with Lyndon Johnson's presidency.

Whether Clinton might have achieved more on behalf of domestic pro-grams is also a subject of growing debate among policy analysts. Politi-cal scientists James MacGregor Burns and Georgia J. Sorenson advance a highly critical but unpersuasive analysis of the Clinton presidency.

They opine, not wrongly, that Clinton failed "to tackle the big changes needed to overcome the most glaring deficiencies and inequalities in American society." In their view, he was not a "transforming leader like Abraham Lincoln and Franklin Roosevelt" but a mere transactional president intent on making deals and promoting "itty-bitty" measures such as family leave or school uniforms. But missing from their biting critique of Clinton's centrist politics and agenda is a sense of realism about what was politically possible during his presidency. Unlike Lincoln or Roosevelt, he faced no historic crisis of the magnitude of the Civil War, the Great Depression, or World War II. At the same time, the country had little stomach for big government spending programs or initiatives, especially after the GOP victory in 1994. Yet by pushing for deficit reduction and small-scale programs that the country favored, Clinton managed to survive and fight another day, thereby opening the door to the broader agendas of his second term.

Historian Garry Wills offers a more balanced and perceptive appraisal. He sees Clinton as having protected government at a time when the momentum was with the Republican leaders determined to roll back government and weaken, if not destroy, the welfare state. Wills also understands the limits of what could be done in a politically conservative era. At least Clinton's approach to governing offered a plausible way to achieve something in Congress, as illustrated by his successful effort to improve and broaden the earned income tax credit for the working poor. In addition, Clinton's use of executive authority advanced, among other items, a progressive agenda with regard to the environment and appointments. And his many vetoes also prevented considerable Republican legislation, designed to weaken government and the welfare state, from becoming law.

Of considerable importance, too, was Clinton's role in shaping the national Democratic Party. As a New Democrat, he successfully repositioned it on matters affecting crime, welfare, and budgets. But his legacy was mixed as he failed to reorient the party's foreign trade policy, as evidenced by a majority of Democratic votes in the House in opposition to NAFTA and normalizing trade with China.

Clinton was also very lucky. During his eight years in the White House, the country experienced an unprecedented economic boom and faced no serious external threat. The economy produced phenomenal new wealth for some, though a majority of workers hardly shared in the economic surge. Yet it is hard to imagine in the prevailing political climate what Clinton might have done about developments that further enhanced the persistent inequality in the American economic system. Nevertheless, during his tenure as president, millions entered the labor market for the first time and found work. The economy benefited Clinton in many ways. He won the presidency in 1992 because of high unemployment, and he was reelected in 1996 thanks to an increasingly good economy. He also survived impeachment because a majority gave him consistently high job approval ratings as the good times continued to roll. Whether Clinton's economic policies actually laid the foundation for that boom is difficult to determine and will be the subject of further analysis and discussion in the years to come.

Abroad, Clinton accepted the reality of globalization and pushed hard for further American integration into the new, more fully interdependent world of global markets and capital flows. His efforts to win congressional ratification of the NAFTA treaty and the normalization of trade with China reflected this commitment. On the other hand, not until after the Asian economic crisis of 1997 did he mention the need for a new international "architecture" to cope with the possibility of a global economic meltdown and the rapidly increasing disparity in wealth and resources between the First World and the rest of humankind. Nor did he say much about the concerns of labor leaders and environmentalists, worried about the consequences of unfettered globalization, until street demonstrations erupted against the World Trade Organization in Seattle in December 1999.

Certainly Clinton made a major effort to find peaceful solutions to the agonizing conflicts in Northern Ireland and the Middle East. He also engaged in war in Kosovo, hoping to prevent a repeat of the ethnic cleansing that had already occurred in Bosnia. He tried to keep the door open with Russia, saying little about either its brutal invasion of Chechnya or the massive internal corruption of the Yeltsin regime. But Clinton failed to win Senate ratification of the Comprehensive Test Ban Treaty, a major defeat of historic proportions. On another important matter, he decided not to give the go-ahead for the construction of a limited defensive missile shield, which both Russia and China, along with many NATO allies, strongly opposed. Thus, he left to the next president the responsibility for deciding either to move ahead with the project or, possibly, to halt it altogether.

The Clinton presidency was not an important presidency as were, say, Ronald Reagan's and Franklin Roosevelt's. Still, Clinton was a gifted politician of high intelligence who came to power at a time when liberalism remained in deep crisis. Caught in the middle of a power struggle between Democratic liberals and Republican conservatives, he spent precious political resources fending off both sides, with each opposing him for different reasons. Liberals had good reason to believe that he made deals with Republicans at their expense, particularly with regard to welfare, foreign trade, and the deficit. Conservatives despised him, thinking, mistakenly, that he was a radical from the 1960s generation.

Yet while he moved incrementally toward an amorphous center, Clinton advanced an agenda that took into account the need for greater tolerance and justice for gays, blacks, and Hispanic Americans. He helped protect a woman's right to an abortion from congressional sanctions. And he promoted pathbreaking environmental measures. He weakened civil liberties by signing the Counter-Terrorism Act, which "imported into our law the loathsome practice of trials on secret evidence." In addition, he put his signature on a welfare bill that went far to make life harder and more difficult for single mothers and their children.

Whether the efforts of William Jefferson Clinton constituted a revival of liberalism or a continuation of conservatism, or a mix of the two, will be a question at the heart of future studies seeking to determine his rightful place in the pantheon of American presidents.

Bibliographical Essay

Although the Clinton historiography is at the earliest stage of development, many published books, along with material from the *New York Times*, *Washington Post*, *Wall Street Journal*, *New York Review of Books*, and *Nation*, form the factual foundation on which this survey rests.

Among them is William C. Berman's *America's Right Turn: From Nixon to Clinton, 2nd Ed.* (Baltimore: Johns Hopkins University Press, 1998), which provides an overview and analysis of the conservative resurgence in American politics. E. J. Dionne's *Why Americans Hate Politics* (New York: Simon & Schuster, 1991) is a thoughtful and readable work worth consulting. Benjamin Ginsberg and Martin Shefter's *Politics by Other Means: Politicians, Prosecutors, and the Press from Watergate to Whitewater* (New York: Norton, 1999) is a penetrating critique of the political and governmental system that helped to shape the Clinton presidency.

There are a number of excellent biographies of Clinton, focusing on his career before he moved to Washington. An outstanding work is David Maraniss's *First in His Class: The Biography of Bill Clinton* (New York: Simon & Schuster, 1995). See also John Brummett's *Highwire: From the Back Roads to the Beltway—The Education of Bill Clinton* (New York: Hyperion, 1994). An important study bearing on Clinton's political career is Kenneth Baer's *Reinventing Democrats: The Politics of Liberalism from Reagan to Clinton* (Lawrence: University Press of Kansas, 2000). For a balanced analysis of the 1992 election, see *The Election of 1992: Reports and Interpretations*, ed. Gerald M. Pomper (Chatham, N.J.: Chatham House, 1993).

Journalist Elizabeth Drew's works provide a fund of information on and insights into the first Clinton administration. See *On the Edge: The Clinton Presidency* (New York: Simon & Schuster, 1995) and *Showdown: The Struggle between the Gingrich Congress and the Clinton White House* (New York: Simon & Schuster, 1997). Bob Woodward's *The Agenda* (New York: Simon & Schuster, 1994) focuses on the story of deficit reduction during the early months of the Clinton presidency. For many valuable articles on public policy issues during the first Clinton administration, see *The Social Divide: Political Parties and the Future of Activist Government*, ed. Margaret Weir (Washington, D.C.: Brookings, 1998). For similarly good material but from a somewhat different perspective, see also *Social Policy and the Conservative Agenda*, ed. Clarence Y. H. Lo and Michael Schwartz (Malden, Mass.: Blackwell, 1998).

Jacob Hacker's *The Road to Nowhere: The Genesis of President Clinton's Plan for Health Care* (Princeton: Princeton University Press, 1997) is a first-class monograph. Daniel Patrick Moynihan includes a critique of the Clintons' health plan in *Miles To Go: A Personal History of Social Policy* (Cambridge: Harvard University Press, 1997). E. J. Dionne explores how and why the Republicans captured Congress in 1994 in his stimulating *They Only Look Dead: Why Progressives Will Dominate the Next Political Era* (New York: Simon & Schuster, 1995). See also *Midterm: The Elections of 1994 in Context*, ed. Philip Klinker (Boulder, Colo.: Westview, 1996). James MacGregor Burns and Georgia J. Sorenson's *Dead Center: Clinton–Gore Leadership and the Perils of Moderation* (New York: Scribner, 1999) combines good material with a flawed analysis.

Former Secretary of Labor Robert Reich and Clinton policy adviser George Stephanopoulos have each published their memoirs. Reich's *Locked in the Cabinet* (New York: Knopf, 1997) reveals much about the major domestic priorities of the first Clinton administration. Stephanopoulos's *All Too Human: A Political Education* (Boston: Little, Brown, 1999) spells out his increasing frustration working for a president who ignored his advice. Dick Morris's *Behind the Oval Office: Winning the Presidency in the Nineties* (New York: Random House, 1997) is required reading for all students of Clinton's presidency. James Stewart's *Blood Sport: The President and His Adversaries* (New York: Simon & Schuster, 1996) is a detailed study of the Whitewater controversy. James Ceaser and Andrew Busch provide a sound analysis of the background to and the results of the 1996 election in *Losing to Win: The 1996 Elections and American Politics* (Lanham, Md.: Rowman & Littlefield, 1997).

Thomas Palley, in *Plenty of Nothing: The Downsizing of the American Dream and the Case for Structural Keynesianism* (Princeton: Princeton University Press, 1998), discusses the impact of NAFTA on American workers. Taylor Dark explores organized labor's relationship with the Democratic Party in *The Unions and the Democrats: An Enduring Alliance* (Ithaca: Cornell University Press, 1999). William Greider's *One World, Ready or Not: The Manic Logic of Global Capitalism* (New York: Simon & Schuster, 1998) is an important book illuminating the complex political and economic trends of globalization. Edward Wolff offers a nuanced analysis of wealth distribution in the United States in *Top Heavy: The Increasing Inequality of Wealth in America and What Can Be Done about It* (New York: New Press, 1995).

William Hyland's *Clinton's World: Remaking American Foreign Policy* (Westport, Conn.: Praeger, 1999) surveys the foreign policy initiatives and dilemmas of the Clinton presidency. See also Wayne Burt's *Reluctant Superpower: United States Policy in Bosnia* (New York: St. Martin's, 1997). Indispensable is Tim Judah's superb *Kosovo: War and Revenge* (New Haven: Yale University Press, 2000).

Elizabeth Drew narrates, in fitting fashion, the story of money and politics in *The Corruption of American Politics: What Went Wrong and Why* (Secaucus, N.J.: Birch Lane, 1999). Richard Posner provides a subtle overview and analysis of the Clinton impeachment controversy in *An Affair of State: The Investigation, Impeachment, and Trial of President Clinton* (Cambridge: Harvard University Press, 1999). Jeffrey Toobin writes from a very different perspective in *A Vast Conspiracy: The Real Story of the Sex Scandal That Nearly Brought Down a President* (New York: Random House, 2000). Christopher Hitchens's *No One Left to Lie To: The Triangulations of William Jefferson Clinton* (New York: Verso, 1999), is a pointed critique.

Of the many articles and essays consulted for this survey, a number stand out for their special importance. Joe Klein's "Eight Years: Bill Clinton Looks Back on His Presidency," in the *New Yorker*, October 16–23, 2000, is an excellent brief introduction to the politics and policies of the Clinton presidency. Lars-Erik Nelson's several essays in the *New York Review of Books* provide a thoughtful commentary on the Clinton presidency. See, for example, his "The Republicans' War,"

NYRB, February 4, 1999; "Undemocratic Vistas," *NYRB*, August 12, 1999; and "Clinton and His Enemies," *NYRB*, January 20, 2000. Louis Uchitelle's many *New York Times* articles analyzing the state of the American economy during the Clinton years are insightful. See, for example, his "107 Months, and Counting," *NYT*, January 30, 2000, Section 3; and "U.S. Productivity Rose at 5% Rate in 2nd Half of 99," *NYT*, February 9, 2000. Garry Wills's "The Clinton Principle," in the *New York Times Magazine*, January 19, 1997, examines Clinton's concept of government in the post-Reagan era. Stanley Kutler's "Resignation, No; Impeachment, Maybe," in the *Los Angeles Times*, September 14, 1998, discusses the important constitutional stakes involved in a possible Clinton resignation. Historian Leo Ribuffo illuminates the continuities of American history by placing the Clinton presidency in the broad context of twentieth-century progressivism. See "From Carter to Clinton: The Latest Crisis of American Liberalism," *American Studies International*, June 1997.

Index

About the Author

William Berman received his Ph.D. from Ohio State University. A specialist in post-1945 political history and public policy issues, he taught American history at the California State College of Pennsylvania, the University of Louisville, and for nearly thirty years at the University of Toronto, where he is now Professor Emeritus. Among his publications are *The Politics of Civil Rights in the Truman Administration, William Fulbright and the Vietnam War: The Dissent of a Political Realist,* and *America's Right Turn: From Nixon to Clinton.*

4375640